Poetry in Balance

Erasmus Cromwell-Smith II

Poetry in Balance
© Erasmus Cromwell-Smith II

ISBN: 979-8-9873115-5-4
Publisher: RCHC LLC
Editor: Elisa Arraiz Lucca
Cover Design, and Interior Design:
erasmuscromwellsmith
Printed in USA, 2022

Books written by the author

In English,	En Español,
As Erasmus Cromwell-Smith II:	**Como Erasmus Cromwell-Smith II:**
- The Equilibrist series,	-La serie del Equilibrista,
(Inspirational/Philosophical)	(Inspiracional/Filosófico)
- The Happiness Triangle (Vol. 1)	- El triángulo de la felicidad (Vol. 1)
- Geniality (Vol. 2)	- Genialidad (Vol. 2)
- The Magic in Life (Vol. 3)	- La magia de la vida (Vol. 3)
- Poetry in Equilibrium	- Poesía en equilibrio
- The Equilibrist (Trilogy)	- El Equilibrista (La serie completa)
(Young Adults)	**(Jóvenes Adultos)**
-The Orloj of Prague (Vol. 1)	-El Orloj de Praga (Vol. 1)
-The Orloj of Venice (Vol. 2)	-El Orloj de Venecia (Vol. 2)
-The Orloj of Paris (Vol. 3)	-El Orloj de Paris (Vol. 3)
-The Orloj of London (Vol. 4)	-El Orloj de Londres (Vol. 4)
-The Orloj of Boston (Vol. 5)	-El Orloj de Boston (Vol. 5).
-Poetry in Balance	-Poesía en Balance
As Erasmus Cromwell-Smith II	**Como Erasmus Cromwell-Smith II**
The South Beach Conversational Method	**El Método Conversacional South Beach**
(Educational)	(Educacional)
-Spanish	-Inglés
-German	-Alemán
-French	-Francés
-Italian	-Italiano
-Portuguese	-Portugués
The Nicolas Tosh Series,	**La serie de Nicolás Tosh,**
(Sci-fi)	**(Ciencia ficción)**
- Algorithm-323	- Algoritmo -323
- Algorithm-325	- Algoritmo-325
- Algorithm-326	- Algoritmo-326
As Nelson Hamel (*)	**Como Nelsón Hamel (*)**
The Paradise Island Series,	**La serie de la isla paraíso**
(Action Thriller)	(Acción Suspenso)
-Miami Beach, Dangerous Liaisons	-Miami Beach, Relaciones peligrosas
The Rebel Hackers Series,	**La Serie de los Hackers Rebeldes,**
(Sci-fi)	(Ciencia Ficción)
-The Rebel Hackers of Point Breeze	-Los Hackers Rebeldes de Point Breeze
-The Rebel Hackers of the Glacial Dawn	-Los Hackers rebeldes del amanecer glacial
-Threshold of Embodiment	- Umbral de la encarnación

(*) in collaboration with Charles Sibley.

All titles are or will be available in audio book

Author's Note

My intent has been to craft artful verses that are straightforward, easy to understand. The emphasis has been on the message, not on getting the reader lost in the traditional intricacies, metrics even incomprehensible abstractions of traditional poetry. Through art that speaks to all, I seek to elicit emotions while provoking reflection. Verses that jump with ease out of the pages of a book, enrapturing anyone's heart. By writing free verse as if it was a meaningful conversation among friends, I've aimed to break the common apathy or predisposition towards poetry in general. On every theme, I asked myself many times over, the following questions:

Am I passionate enough about this subject matter?
- Is my vision on the subject somehow different than the norm?
- Can I articulate it through art?
- Have I educated myself sufficiently about each particular source of inspiration?
- Can I write something that could be interpreted and experienced in different dimensions?
- Can I compose versatile poetry that is as light or as deep as the reader may want it to be?
- Can I create a verse that inspires, impacts, even heals others?

If the answers to all these questions were affirmative, I embarked into meditative and introspective journeys searching for the next magic creative moment. From then on, visualization coupled with sensing of the subject matter unleashed torrents of words that became a poem, a fable, an essay, or a scribble.

The poetry, the fables and short stories draws a circle of life, covering existential ground that brings along, inspirational, emotional, and spiritual enrichment to an otherwise mundane life.

"Poetry in Balance" is dedicated to all those poetry lovers that want to experience the series prose without a storyline or a plot framing it. As a special treat, at the end of the book, I've included a set of sci-fi poems, existential in nature, as reflection to the conundrum, and intersection between technology, artificial intelligence and humankind.

Erasmus Cromwell-Smith II.

TABLE OF CONTENTS

"The Weakness of Insulting Others"

We insult others when feeling less
than them or the situation we face.
Even though on the surface,
pejoratives appear to be directed at others,
what they reflect in reality,
is anger at ourselves,
out of feelings of inferiority,
perhaps frustrated at our incapacity
in a given moment
or reckoning with mediocrity.

Cursing others is also driven
by fear of being ousted
and our weaknesses noticed or our insecurities
about losing or not prevailing.
We put others down,
when artificially,
we try to feel better or superior to them,
when in reality
we see them being better than us.

When we insult others
what we are really doing
in the final analysis,
is insulting ourselves.

When in the reflection of our conscience
in vain we try to believe,
there is a reflection of others
when in reality it is only us,
staring right back
and at no one else.

"Patience"

Knowing how,
and knowing when to wait,
are the essences of patience.

Patience allows us
to slow things down,
as well as,
to control
abrupt-impulsive behavior.

Patience is a character quality
that requires
bountiful wisdom,
profound maturity,
absolute inner-peace,
immutable self-control
and total calmness.

Patience is a virtue
that provides us
with the best shot
at having "The Right Timing"
for anything
or anyone.

Patience is the best existential tool,
to "Cool Things Down,"
before we act
in the spur of the moment,

perhaps enabling us,
to realize mistakes or errors,
which we may be about to incur.

Patience is a deliberate
"Lapse" in time
between Willingness and Action,
Rushing and Pausing,
Winning and Losing,
being Happy and Smiling,
regretting Sadly
and having Second Chances.

When we are besieged
by impatience,
it's sound to remember,
that in nature,
Morning will come,
Night will follow,
The Sun will rise
and at Day's End,
it'll reset all over again,
while moving alongside,
Nature's inexorable beat.

Everything happens in the Universe
for a reason
and at the right moment,
not a speck of time sooner,
not a fraction of a second later.

And there's always
a Cosmic or Divine reason
for time to behave in such a way.

But, above all
Nature as its core
cannot be altered,
much less,
pushed, forced, or sped-up.

Patience is, therefore,
an existential requirement,
as we chase and follow,
The Beat, Pace, Tics, and Rhythm
of Life itself;
Along with Nature, The Cosmos,
and
The Universe as a whole.

"An Upside-Down World"

The young girl protests. "Nothing works in here!"

Professes her mentor. "That is obvious and yet, not quite the way to think."

She asks impatiently. "How can I open any door?"

Quickly asserts her mentor. "By closing it."

She asks incredulously. "What about climbing a flight of stairs?"

Her mentor confirms while showing infinite patience.
"You can do that, but only by going down first."

The young woman asks in turmoil.
"How do you do that, without being able to climb them first?"

He lectures with precision. "That's for you to figure out."

She declares in despair. "I can't. I'm paralyzed."

Her mentor confirms in resignation. "Yes, you are."

She declares while totally lost. "Don't know what to do."

Declares the young's girl's mentor steering her towards the wisdom of it all.
"Actually, knowing you don't know, is a belief in itself."

She states trying to evade her predicament. "I am hungry."

Her mentor clarifies once more, with no logic at hand.
"In here the only way to satisfy your hunger is by not eating."

She asks in contempt. "What kind of a place is this?"

Her mentor responds while staying on course.
"One where nothing is what it seems."

The young woman babbles in disgust, but she is just trying desperately to put on a brave face.
"I am sick and tired of your silly games."

Silence conveying obliviousness and obviousness ensues.

The young woman quibbles, rhetorically, all by herself.
"Wait a minute, don't tell me that in order to take a shower, I simply don't, right?"

A relieved mentor states, recognizing the sudden progress of his mentee.
"The wisdom of absurdity has begun to enlighten you, young apprentice."

The young woman vents.
"I am glad you see it that way because what I feel right now is contempt, sarcasm, and utter frustration."

The mentor further drives his point across.
"All you are doing is rejecting change."

Sarcastically the young woman asks.
"What about this conversation, how come we are having it?"

Her "cynical deafness" is finally uncovered.

She says in realization.
"Oh, I get it we are not having this conversation. This conversation is not happening."

The mentor affirms, correcting her once more.
"No, to the contrary, we are indeed having one."

She claims realizing that she still doesn't have a clue.
"What do you mean, I am totally confused."

The mentor asserts as the lesson inexorably takes hold of his mentee.
"Our conversation exists, simply it is a non-conversation."

The young woman vents again without conviction.
"This is all highly irritating."

Her mentor declares, sensing that he finally has his mentee's total attention.
"What is unnerving you is that nothing in here is how it's supposed to be or what you are used to. Change makes you so uncomfortable, that you resist or oppose it, not deliberately but viscerally."

The young woman disagrees, but only half-heartedly.
"I think you got it all wrong, I simply am skeptical by nature."

Her mentor further explains as she nods her head in consent and agreement, for the first time.
"No, that's a separate problem. Besides fear to change, you are rattled inside because you see the world in a certain way. You have a prescribed knowledge about how things work. To find out that such perception may be erroneous completely unsettles and frustrates you. Your defense mechanisms and survival instincts are set in motion, your reaction is the denial of that which discredits your vision of the truth and your belief systems."

She asks with a genuine desire to learn.
"Why am I irritated then?"

"Erroneously, what you really feel, is inadequate in the situation you face and your interaction with people. That places you in a position of inferiority when handling the circumstances you find yourself in. Thus, your reaction of anger or irritation is nothing but a protective shield, a defense mechanism. Your sarcasm and skepticism are only a reflection of how you feel about yourself. You respond by lashing out and criticizing or insulting others. Sadly, you're doing it out of feelings of inadequacy, inferiority, and frustration with yourself as you reject change."

"The Young Boy and The Lion"

Along the Zambezi River he walks, the young boy from Zimbabwe.
The sudden roar freezes him.
Right on his back, a mighty lion seizes his prey,
A second roar follows, it is quieter and deliberate as if in slow motion,
Kunte senses the lion as tension builds up,
'He is ready to attack,' the young boy reasons.
Kunte turns around enough to see the fiery look in the king of the jungle's eyes.

It is precisely at that moment when the Words of Wisdom of Yeti, his mentor and the tribe's conjurer, come to use.

"Kunte, the key to bond with the wild beast is to control your fear and to show humility."

While staring at the lion, the young boy slowly bows his head.
The effect is immediate as the lion seems to relax and does not move forward.

Then to Kunte's great surprise, without taking his eyes off the young boy, the magnificent beast lowers himself and lies down on the ground.

Having heard both roars, Yeti fears the worst, so, he runs desperately through the bush, in search of his beloved mentee.

As he sees the river come closer, there they are, staring at each other, the young boy and the lion.

The wild animal immediately senses Yeti and turns his head towards him.

The frantic fear in the eyes of the conjurer crosses the calm eyes of the beast.

The lion tenses and stands up.

A frightening roar follows.

Yeti stops right in his tracks and prepares for the worst as he is in the crosshairs of the wild animal.

That's when an amazing and magical moment happens...

The young boy takes a step forward and the lion immediately turns around towards him.

The body language of the beast announces a roar, the head and the jaw make the movements, but there is no sound coming out of the lion.

With his head still bowed and an extended arm reaching out,
Kunte continues to approach step by step the mighty king of the jungle.

Yeti, the old conjurer, is overcome by emotion and a couple of tears slide down his cheeks as he sees Kunte, the young boy, first pat, then hug with his two arms and finally kiss the beautiful lion.

"The Kite Flyer and the Wise Old Master"

With the snow-capped Himalayas as a background,
the wise old master, though he seems restless and uneasy,
still exudes the awareness of a focused good observer.

He has closely cropped white hair,
a round face with a sparse mustache,
a tiny mouth with barely noticeable lips,
intense eyes filled with serenity and wisdom.

The boy he is keeping an eye on,
flies a kite reaching high up into the sky,
bright and shiny colors it has,
swirls with the winds of Annapurna,
climbs in a frenzy and dives in every direction,
at the mercy of its diminutive handler.

"It is never fast enough," complains the little boy with a grin on
his face.

Suddenly,
the winds from the menacing mountain arrive and the show is
over quickly.

"Another dud," protests the boy from Nepal, as he picks-up his
crashed paper mâché, flying object.

Standing at the doorstep of his modest residence, the wise old
master is not pleased.

The young boy comes running and sits on the rocky dirt, beside
his mentor.

"Let me take a look at your kite," the Wisemaster says.
With quick and highly skilled movements, in no time, the
craftsman's hands tinker, cut and paste, rendering the kite in top
shape, ready in no time to fly again.

The youth bows in gratitude at the stern face of the old master.

"Try it now, Tenzing," he commands.

The young boy quickly runs away against the wind while deftly
pulling the strings.

The kite promptly soars, higher and faster than ever before, it
rides the winds of the mountain of heaven with ease, drawing
perfectly elliptical paths, and wide circles in its wake.

But once again, the boy does not smile,
much less so his wise mentor.

"All other kites at our village are either faster
 or better than mine,"
he blurts out while talking to himself.

"Besides, for all of us, the kids of this town, it is pointless to fly
kites, against the winds of the monster mountain."

"Tenzing come over here!" demands the exasperated Wisemaster.

After picking up his, once again, newly smashed kite, the young
boy runs right to his mentor's doorstep.

"What is it with your restless soul?" the old master asks.

"My kite is useless," responds the young Nepalese boy.

He wears a frustrated expression, while standing next to his
broken and inert flying object lying on the dirt.

"We'll see about that," the wise man asserts.

After repairing the kite, while deftly pulling the strings, he takes a few quick steps, instantly lifting the kite into the blue sky.

Like an arrow piercing through the air, the kite flies at a frantic pace, at gravity defying angles, perilously dangerous curves, lopsided turns, jet engine elevators, speed of light simulators.

"Wisemaster, how can you do it?"
The Nepalese youngster asks, as the old man continues to pilot the kite as if it was on a racetrack.

Kite on his shoulder, its tail being dragged behind,
with the freezing winds of Annapurna now howling,
the young Sherpa walks alongside the wise old man,
as they head towards the mountain temple,
where their daily mentoring sessions take place.

"Tenzing, you missed the magnificent flight of your kite,"
the Wisemaster observes while adding,
"You were concentrating within your mind so much on the imperfections, that the joyful ride totally escaped you."

"Master, what should I have done then?"
Asks the perplexed young boy.

"Do not obsess any longer on what you are lacking but only on what you do have, whatever that is," the Wisemaster replies.

"Immersed in your never-ending grievances, you are not enjoying the journey," he continues.

The old man paces with pensive strides.

"Look up!" He suddenly commands
while the young boy jumps in obedience.

"See, glorious, cloudless skies.
A gift, a privilege to be enjoyed.
In life as we march along, it is rewarding when we are aware of
our surroundings and paying attention.
It is evidently worthwhile to view the sides, and both before and
behind, because at every turn, there are lofty existential treasures
waiting for us at every turn," the Wisemaster adds.

"Now breathe deep," the old man orders the young man.

Tenzing does as instructed, filling his lungs with fresh air.

"You see, while you argue and complain which constricts your
veins, not enough oxygen is inhaled,
to pump life into your being,"
notes the wise old master.

Tenzing lowers his head in embarrassment,
but the wise man is not done yet.

"My beloved mentee, you always find the need to compare
yourself or what you have; the kites of others are always better
than yours. You constantly aspire for what others are or have,
hence, you are perennially unhappy, deeply in fact,"
 states the old man in a reflective trance.

"But there is an additional existential disease
that rots your insides,
including your spirit and soul: Excuses and more excuses.
Today you blamed the mountain's winds, but all you did was to
complain trying to hide your lack of mastery."

"Your kite piloting skills are limited.
You denigrate your kite so often and so much,
that you are never in a position
to extract the most out of what it can do.
You complain and protest so frequently, while operating it,
that you fail to study, learn, and practice,
which are the only ways to advance in life.
Hence, there is no progress for you as a pilot.
Your lack of mastery is a consequence of your lack of effort,
that condemns one to a life of mediocrity,"
the emotional Wisemaster adds.

"I've just flown your kite.
What was the difference between you and me?
After all, it was the same kite, the same weather
and the same location," the old man emotionally exclaims.

The young apprentice reacts,
"You were totally focused on the moment,
therefore, able to extract the most out of my kite."

The Wisemaster remarks in exaltation, "Exactly!"

"You enjoyed the flight, the kite, the surroundings
and above all, you enjoyed the journey,
even though, you were aware that none of them were perfect,"
responds the suddenly inspired young man.

"Wonderful! You're beginning to understand,"
states a jubilant old man.

"You paid no attention to appearances,
neither kites others may have, much less the trying weather,"
concludes the smiling young man.

"Tenzing, you are now ready to become a master of what you love to do. Go, go and enjoy the ride," states the Wisemaster.

The young Nepalese boy runs with his kite; when ready,
still holding the strings, he releases it to fly, high up into the sky,
it sails masterfully, with a now deft touch;
the biggest triumph though,
is that he wears a bright big wide smile,
that goes along quite fittingly,
with the magnificent event,
he's experiencing while maneuvering his kite
in front of his venerable mentor.

"The Old Man and Mother Nature"

While a new day begins
in between the jagged edges
of the snowcapped mountains,
the sun breaks on the horizon.

The old man drags himself up
step by step
as he grudgingly labors
up the steep mountain hike.

Every one of his bones
makes creaking noises
hurting as he moves.

A beautiful forest surrounds him
while the path he follows
zig zags endlessly through the slow climb.

His little sac bounces on his back,
his precious midway meal lies in there.

The steep terrain opens up
as he leaves the dense foliage behind.

The landscape is now a plateau
composed of mountain peaks
illustrating the background.

While he ascends

over a narrow way of loose flat stones,
the terrain is carpeted
with wildflowers and kneecap grass.

Above him, there isn't a single cloud in the sky
but only intense and stunning hues of blue
acting as his heavenly ceiling.
The summit is the reward
for an effort that has lasted for many hours.

At the top of the mountain lies a deep blue lake,
on its side lies an elongated waterfall
that frames and trickles into it.

On his back, he can see the valley where he started.
The panoramic alpine views
allow him to see a blurry image
of his village from afar,
miles and miles away.

"I am short of breath
and my mouth is so dry,
I can hardly swallow."
He announces seemingly to no one.

"Besides, my runny nose and watery eyes
are trying to tell me
that my allergies are running amuck."
he continues talking all to himself
as he walks towards the top.

Then, as always happens,
the thunderous voice permeates all over,
the sound waves can be felt everywhere.

"How do you like the smell of the forest
you are climbing?"
Asks mother nature of the old man.

"Same as always,
but right now I'm gasping for air
afflicted by my summer allergies."
He answers with a cranky voice.

"Discomfort is compensated by a gorgeous day
and the stunning colors
of the flowers, butterflies, autumn leaves
and a clear blue sky all around you."
Nature counters.

"From you, as expected,
besides, what good is it?
So much beauty if I can't enjoy it."
Is the cursory answer from the old man.

"What about the sounds of the wind
brushing and whistling through the trees,
the birds singing,
the tiny creek's waters
coursing through downstream,
the wicked Jiminy Crickets
seemingly unlimited,

all members of my perennial open-air orchestra."
Mother nature argues.

"What do you want from me, nature?
Don't you understand that I am having a hard time?
Or is it that you just want me
to magically forget it all
just thinking and feeling
only about 'the nice things in life?'"
The exasperated old man argues back.

"Precisely, privileged man."
Nature bellows in a stern voice.

"Privileged, are you kidding me?"
He counters with sarcasm.

"Your good health and enduring strength
have made it possible for you to climb
this tough and challenging terrain
all the way to this beautiful summit!"
Mother nature counters unfazed.

Responsively,
"why don't you leave alone
my sorrowfulness and foul mood.
You are not going to persuade me
to cheer up when I don't feel like it."
He attempts,
blocking the uncomfortable weight
of a reality he doesn't want to see or feel.

"You've earned the privilege
to be standing at the pinnacle of the world
with this backdrop of stunning views
all around you
and yet somehow you've found a way
to be unhappy about it,
worst of all,
not even appreciating it."
Mother nature rebuts
in a solemn and stern voice.

The old man remains silent
trying to show indifference
but his eyes are attentive
and seem to be pleading
to mother nature,
not to give up on him.

"Old man, what if
the air you breathe
that I provide for you
every second you are alive,
is suddenly gone?
Or what would happen
if the oceans, rivers, lakes, springs, and wells
were to dry out in an instant?
Or if the protective shield of our planet
were to vanish in a split second?
Why do you take for granted
that these boundless gifts

you receive every day
will continue forever?
You have an existential obligation
to give back,
to life and others
for the privilege of being alive."
This is a declaration
by a visibly obfuscated mother nature.

The old man's eyes are filled with intensity
as he's followed every word
mother nature has just uttered.

"And how do I do that?"
He babbles in embarrassment.

"In life, we do that which has been
prescribed, obligated and meant for us to do,
as participants
in the natural order of the universe."

"Sometimes we are at the receiving end,
others on the giving end."
Nature declares with profound wisdom.

"Your generosity unsettles me,
you make me feel uncomfortable around you."

"Perhaps guilty?" Counters nature.

"What does it matter how I feel?
But tell me please,
how can you do all that you do

without receiving anything in return
for your actions?"
An incredulous old man retorts.

"That is what being generous means.
It's about paying forward.
Being giving is not a choice,
it is a debt.
Our existential obligations keep piling up
as long as we remain
the beneficiaries of the privilege
of partaking in this earth."
Adds mother nature sounding calmer
as the attention of the older man rises.

"Be gracious, cheerful
and celebrate the life you enjoy
each and every day
and make it your existential purpose
to gratefully give back as much as you receive.
Don't cause me to change my mindset
and stop giving you all those things
that sustains your life.

Above all, be mindful that
my generosity comes
without any strings attached to it.
I never ask for anything
in return to offset what I give.

Hence, why shouldn't you as well
give back equally so?"

"The Three Bavarian Bakers"

Once upon a time
there were three bakers
in the town of Fürstenfeldbruck
near Munich
in the picturesque
southern German region of Bavaria.

Dieter, Kurt, and Helmut
were childhood friends
and had started baking at an early age
as their neighbor and idol, Hans Neumann,
Dieter's father was the best baker in town.

To their advantage,
he created all of his best recipes
and new creations
in secret at home in a separate building
his "Sanctum Sanctorum"
where he mixed and prepared
all his magic pastes.

His "baking-lab" was already stocked
with all the tools and ingredients, he needed,
including a large oven
that constantly emanated
the magic scent of freshly baked treats.

Before or after school,
while he was at work at his lab,
the three curious kids would peek

at master baker Neumann
when at work
and would run away when he noticed them.

But the sweet aroma
of all kinds of bread, pastries, tarts, and cakes
kept on drawing them back.

The busy baker was always aware of their presence
but he let it be,
as he was not only bemused
by their enchanting childish games
but more importantly
because their persistence reassured him
of their genuine interest in his trade.

One good day when he felt they were ready for it,
he suddenly turned around
and staring intently in their direction
caught them by surprise
as the tightly bunched threesome
peeked through the window.

"There is no need for the three of you to hide."
Mr. Neumann said to the three eight year olds
from his workbench.

"Come in, don't be shy."

The startled youngsters promptly complied
to his command.

Baker Neumann did not disappoint

as the three childhood friends
were promptly treated
with bites of the best tarts, cakes, and pastries
they'd ever eaten in their short lives.

At first, he sat them down to observe as he toiled.
As time went by,
he commenced explaining step by step
not only what baking was all about
but also how he was doing it.

He started to involve them
in the process
so they learned to do it themselves.

Predicatively the three of them
went on to become bakers.

Kurt became a master "baker,"
offering at his location,
more than a hundred different types
of freshly baked bread.

Helmut became famous
as the best cake, tarts, and pies maker in the city,
ranging from weddings to coffee cakes.

Dieter became a "master confectioner"
offering the best pastries in town.

Unfortunately, their success also marked
the end of the friendship
between the three of them,

turning them into
fierce rivals and competitors.

"There is no better bread in Bavaria than yours Kurt,"
says Maria Schmidt, a regular customer,
she is referring
to the more than a hundred types of bread
on display at Kurt's famous bakery.

"The aroma of freshly baked bread,
there is none like yours,
hits me every time I'm near your place.
It simply pulls me in," adds Mrs. Schmidt.

"I agree, there isn't a better baker in South Germany.
I love your black bread,
soft and warm inside, crusty, even hard on the outside.
A slice spread with a natural marmalade
and a piece of Emmental cheese is heavenly for me,"
says Claudia Hoffbecker another of his loyal customers.

"Thank you, ladies,
your praise is definitely undeserved,"
Kurt replies politely.

But his mind is somewhere else.

'What good is it for me to be deemed the best baker in town
when the passion and profits of this business
can only be found in cakes and pastries,'
complains Kurt.

As usual,

the waiting line extends around the corner
of Helmut's Cake and Coffee Shop.

"Every few weeks on a Saturday
we drive all the way from Stuttgart
to enjoy Helmut's cakes. We love them,"
Brigitte Muller states passionately.

"We actually buy two or three at a time
so at home, we can always have some.
But nothing compares to enjoying them here,
warm, freshly made, just out of the oven,"
states Angela Schlushe to her close friend.

From his office window, Helmut contemplates
his customers patiently waiting in line.
His face though,
does not show either satisfaction or joy.

"What's the point of having so much loyalty and passion
coming from my customers
if all the money is made on bread, pastries, and sweets."

Across town, Ulrich enjoys a "Rote Grutze" dessert
with lots of white cream sauce,
Franz is delighted to taste the warm "ApfelStrudel"
blended in his mouth with Swiss vanilla ice cream.

"Hey, Dieter, pastries craftsman,
what's up with your rivals
Kurt the bread maker and Helmut the cake maker?
Tell me, are they better than you?
Dieter's old friend Ulrich sternly asks

as he is now having a cappuccino...

"No, not at all, we are all masters at our own trade,"
Dieter replies.

"So what's the problem then?" Interjects his friend, Franz.

"They both suffer from the same affliction.
They do not know how to enjoy their success.
Among other things,
they spend most of their time
not only criticizing what others do,
but even worst, comparing and envying
what others have and they don't.
As a result, they are never happy,"

Dieter reflects insightfully.

"The Wounded Tiger"

He hides between the green and yellow leaves,
his muscular and massive body perfectly blended
high-above the branches of the majestic tree,
one of only a handful around
as the bush's grounds look scorched
by the intense heat.

The powerful muscular beast in hiding
lays in wait ready to attack.
He is restless, impatient, and overly thirsty,
his mouth and throat are utterly dry.

But he is hungry and that clouds his instincts.
At this moment, his sole focus of attention
is on a young gazelle, playing in the vicinity,
separated from the herd
unwittingly getting closer and closer
to the tiger's kill zone.

Unbeknownst to the hunting tiger
he is about to be hunted as well.
The two riflemen have him in their sights
with their long-range weapons
aiming straight at him.

Then, both actions happen simultaneously,
the tiger moves ever so slightly ready to jump,
the shooters fire at the same time.
Both shots miss and the tiger takes off

in full knowledge that he is running for his life.

While the panicking tiger scuds away,
his speed is frantic, chaotic, and precipitous.

The shooters manage to get two more rounds off
when the beautiful animal is almost out of range.
One shot misses, the second only grazes his back.

But although causing a slight stumble,
it does not slow him down,
and a split second later, he is gone.

Eventually, at last,
after a seemingly endless run,
the wounded tiger makes his way back to the pack.

He lies down and right after a few pants and moans,
passes out, while a trickle of bright red blood
slowly makes its half-way through his torso and unto his legs.

A couple of females approach him
and start licking his wound,
a band of youngsters does the same
but only the little cubs can reach
his blood-stained legs with their tongues,
they eagerly lick the tasty red liquid.

"Maybe this time, we'll get rid of him for good."

"I sincerely hope your wishes come true."

"I am sick and tired of this super-hero among us."

"Perhaps we should all move and get out of here."

"The hunters may be chasing him."

"And abandon him here?"

"Who cares? He may not make it anyhow."

"It is quite dark already. They will be gone by now,
too dangerous in the dark for them
as they can easily become the hunted,
besides, we don't leave any of us behind."

Suddenly,
a small commotion of grunts
signals something abnormal.
A couple of tigers from another pack
hesitantly approach the wounded tiger.

Everyone is alert and tense,
ready to fight.
But the marauding tigers are not
in an attacking mode.

They slightly bump the females over to the side,
and they all stand aside albeit reluctantly
although remaining close by.

42

The visitors start to lick the wound intensely,
even appearing to suck out the wound's blood.

Next, one of the visiting tigers
brushes his paw with a white chalk
for a split second
over the wound
and shortly thereafter, they are gone.

The following morning the tiger wakes up
and starts to walk gingerly around,
his wound on the mend,
he is getting ready to soon go hunting
once again.

"The Gold Men from Cuzco"

Julio Velazco-Piana and Ramón Ernesto Soto-Duarte bought and sold gold for a living.

Their shops competed fiercely.
Both rivals were strategically located high-up the Andean mountain range at the touristic small town of Cuzco, Peru's getaway to Machu-Pichu, the fabled ancient remains of a city that was once at the heart of the Inca civilization.

Julio's trade was booming.
Over time he had been deft at securing multiple and many sources for his gold.

He promptly paid the best price in the market for what was offered to him.

Hence, almost every gold seller in the region countless individuals and businesses, legitimate or not, went to him.

In addition, he was a master trainer of his trade, with this skill he built in just a few years, the best and most talented stable of gold hand-crafters, all of it resulting in gold jewelry that was by far the highest quality available in the mountain's region, if not perhaps the country.

Peruvian and foreign tourists loved his shop, buyers from all sorts of life and places came to him to buy his gold products.
Ramón Ernesto on the other hand was much more modest in his practice and aspirations, so he bought less and paid more for the gold, resulting in a significantly smaller offering of gold products,

all of it resulting in sales that was easily ten times less than his competitor, Julio's operations.

Despite this, the quality of both their jewels and ornaments were pretty similar.

But when profits were accounted for, Ramón Ernesto, with a significantly smaller and less famous place, made significantly more money than Julio.

Simply by being a lot smaller and having fewer expenses even if the gold cost him more, it cost Ramón Ernesto significantly less to manufacture each piece of jewelry.

Further, when hard times fell on the country, and was accompanied by a steep sales drop Julio had to downsize in a hurry.
Otherwise, he could have gone bust.

Hence the paradox of avarice.
He who covets without limit or moderation, always loses in the long run to the one not possessed by avarice.

"The Academy of the Absurd and the Ignorant"
(including the Outrageous and Ridiculous)

All appears to be normal, as expected and predictable.

Everything seems familiar, known, comfy, but isn't.

The young girl's jolly strides are bouncy, spirited, and carefree. She arrives early, driven by enthusiasm, desire, curiosity. The Academy of Absurdity and Ignorance, baffles her, why does she have to go through this?

What do these people teach? She asks herself drawing a blank.
"If you don't attend and complete their program, you'll be expelled from school," she is told by her high-school principal. "Good Morning, you must be?" States the educational institute's host. "An insurgent teen," replies the young girl.

"A rebel in urgent need of tutelage, I understand," observes the host.
"Sort of..." Blurts inspirited the young girl.
"I gather you are not here voluntarily?" Quizzes rhetorically the host.
"Kind of," babbles the uninterested and restless girl.
"Fair enough, follow me," the eccentric lady instructs.

"What do you teach here?" Asks the puzzled young girl.
"Anything that does not make sense, we study the ridiculous; we learn from the outrageous. We also educate respect to ignorance and reverence to the lack of knowledge. We provide tutelage about the absence of good judgment or the lack of common sense, in other words, we teach absurdity," the peculiar host announces.
"Lead the way please," now fully interested, the restless teen says.

The young girl's full face grimace is followed by a wrinkled brow. in other words, a conspicuously frowned rictus. "Since you are a

46

rebel, the teachings you'll receive here should all be Taylor-made for you."

"Why?"

"Everything taught to you in here will be things that don't make any sense, in other words, it'll be only about that what you love."

"But if these are all bad things, why would anyone teach them?"

"We teach the absurd, outrageous and ridiculous to learn the value of not being like that."

"How could I begin to comprehend such a lesson?" "The principle behind what we teach is that we go in the opposite direction of what is normally taught."

"I'm lost; you have to explain yourself better." "The idea is that if you know about something in depth, you realize its true value or absurdity, you understand its logic or outrageousness, you get its common sense or ridiculousness."

The young rebel girl's eyes brighten as she finally clicks and all the ideas about absurdity and outrageousness inundate and finally reach her.

"If I teach you to respect ignorance either you embrace such aberrant and mediocre behavior or you rebel against and end up rejecting it."

"Hence the value of studying absurdity, outrageousness, and ridiculousness."

"The Young Shepherd and the Tarot Reader"

Early on a Sunday morning, her only free day of the week, the Young Girl pedals down the Arlberg mountains sinuous road. She is coming down to visit the traveling gypsy's caravan. Ever since she can remember, she's been a Sheep Shepherd, so it had her father, grand-father and every other family-head ancestor back in time. All of them male but her, she has broken a deeply rooted tradition of the Austrian Alps.

At an early age her inclination and passion for her father's job had slowly persuaded him that his rightful heir was his precious daughter.

The itinerant traveler's convoy is parked just outside the alpine village.

From afar she can see the vivid colors of the visiting performers' wagons, tents and clothes. Some of the gypsies are dancing, others juggling, one is on a one-wheel cycle, another acrobatic pirouettes.

A small crowd is gathered around each act. The patrons applaud and cheer.

They reward the act with coins and bills, dropping them on the customary hats lying on the floor next to each set of performers.
The Tarot reader's wagon has a long line waiting, the Young Shepherd drops her bike a joins the queue.

Time flies by as she watches the spectacle of street performers. When her turn finally arrives, she is eager and ready.

With trepidation, she climbs the three steps old train wagon.

The incense smell is strong, sweet, and inundates her.

As her eyes adjust to the darkness of the room, she sees her standing with greeting arms and a smile. The Tarot reader is a mane of curly dark hair, cascading over her round face. She has piercing eyes and thick eyebrows. She wears a loose colorful dress, it reaches her ankles and wrists. She has a pair of gigantic rings hanging from her ears. A crystal ball full of smoke sits on a small table next to the Tarot Reader.

"What do we have here? A beautiful young girl from the mountains."
The young Shepherd nods in confirmation.
Gently the Tarot reader picks up the young Shepherd's hands.
"Ah, I see, but you are not a common girl," the Tarot Reader says, "Come dear, have a seat."
She leads the young woman to the small table and they sit. Facing each other, the crystal ball on the side becomes active; gases expand and begin to move within, shades and color tones spread through it.
"Tell me dear, what do you want to know today?"
"What does the future hold for me?"
"For you, anything you may desire."
"For me. How come? Why?"

"You're special."
"Do you tell this to everyone?"
The Tarot Reader smiles but her eyes denote surprise.
"Not quite, Dear, not quite." She says.
"Tell me, beautiful girl, what troubles you about the future?"

"I am a Shepherd and a good one indeed."

"Not only wonderful but a noble profession as well."
"There aren't many women Shepherd's either."
"Are there any at all?" Asks the Tarot Reader.
"I've been told there are a few but I have yet to meet one."

"There you go dear, you are special."

"Well, I wonder if I could be something else."
"Why would you desire so?"
"Sometimes I dream if I could be a writer or perhaps a painter?"
"In life, we can be anything we set our hearts into."
"Will I?" The young Shepherd girl implies staring at the crystal ball.

"Let's take a look," the Tarot Reader says.

"Dear, sometimes our desire to be or do something else is an excuse to escape from the truth."
Gently the Tarot Reader takes the Shepherd's hands and places them on top of the crystal ball. An image of the Alpine country appears on the crystal ball.
"Who's that?" Asks the Tarot Reader.
The young Shepherd girl's mouth is open. Her face denotes total surprise.
"That's my brother."

The Tarot reader rotates her hand around the crystal ball.

The image repeats herself several times at different times and days.
"He has a guilty look," points out the Tarot Reader.

The young Shepherd girl watches the images mesmerized.
"Is he stealing sheep from the herd?"
The young Shepherd nods.

A couple of tears slowly slide down her cheeks.

The Tarot reader moves her hands over the crystal ball again, the images scroll by of the young Shepherd's brother selling the sheep in town. Next, he can be seen on multiple occasions, sitting in a room full of smoke and liquor.

"He's a gambler," The Tarot Reader says.
The young Shepherd woman cries and sobs.

The Tarot Reader once again covers the crystal ball with her hands. It now shows the image of an old man admonishing -in several instances- the young Shepherd woman.
"That's your father and you've taken the blame for your brother on the missing sheep."
The young Shepherd now cries inconsolably. The Tarot Reader stands and embraces her.
"This is the reason you want to know about your future?" The Tarot Reader whispers with a loving tone.
"This is why you wonder if you could be something else?" She adds with tender care in her words.
For the first time the young Shepherd lifts her teary eyes and looks at the Tarot Reader straight in the eyes and nods.
"Well, you've come to the right place my girl," she leans back facing the young Shepherd.
She then takes both her hands again.
"Honesty begins within," she says cryptically.

The young Shepherd girl's eyes grow wide then glow as she begins to understand. "We have first to be honest with ourselves before we preach or profess honesty to others."

The Tarot reader now has the young Shepherd's undivided attention. "You love what you do right?"
"Yes!"

"A Shepherd is what you were born to be. Isn't it right?"
"Absolutely true."
"It's what you've been since an early age." Shyly the young girl nods.
"There's dignity in every legitimate job or profession. There's no valid reason for you to abandon what you love, except dishonesty. You feel ashamed for your sibling's actions, yet you are not truthful

51

with yourself about his bad deeds; you haven't been able to confront him; instead, you've been taking the blame for him. Not being honest with yourself, has led you, to not being honest with your brother or your father, hence perpetuating dishonesty within your family. Your father is upset at you wrongly believing you are at fault, your brother does not respect or fear you, so he continues to steal sheep from your herd. Now to top it all you want to quit and bolt out of the situation thinking that is the solution."

"What do you suggest I do then?"
"First and foremost be honest with yourself. Ask yourself, what is the truth? Spell it out to yourself first. Then go and confront your sibling, demand that he goes and takes full responsibility in front of your father. If he doesn't, go ahead and do it yourself. Also, demand that he pays back the sheep he stole. After all, they don't belong to either of you, they belong to your parents. Once you do this, you'll begin to enjoy being a Shepherd again."

"The Young Seamstress and the Jolly Looking Man"

The young seamstress endlessly spins the wheel driving the spindle, weaving cotton and wool threads of all kinds, thicknesses, and colors.
Sofia labors incessantly day and night.

The young seamstress seeks perfection; her artful creations are sought by many. Whether dresses, cashmeres, cardigans, or scarves, the prodigious seamstress' artisan creations, command a premium and a long wait.

Her prowess is best appreciated by her deftly crochet needlework; done by her at vertiginous speed with a single thread and a pair of long hooked needles.

Yet with all her success, the talented handcrafter obsesses about the past, she is resentful of all of those that at the beginning of her career as seamstress did not believe in her talents and chosen profession nor did they provide support when she needed it the most.

One of the unintended consequences of her painful experiences is that anything Sofia obsesses about; it obfuscates her to no end. Wisely on those moments the young seamstress always takes a break and heads for a stroll on the deep green woods located right off the back of her workshop.

Soon she wanders through the lush nature, trying to take her mind off her grudges.

The sound of the harmonica spreads through the entire forest; It is a soft rhythmic melody.

The faint tune is enchanting;

Its precious notes soothe her. Driven by an irresistible magnetic pull Sofia steps softly over the pine needles.

She doesn't want to disturb the calming effect the melody has on her. Following the source of the comforting tune the young seamstress inches closer and closer -her anger and angst mitigated- cautiously she peeks from the sides of the trunks of the wide-tall trees.

Finally, she sees him sitting on a fallen tree. he's a jolly-looking man with a pleasant expression of happiness plastered all over his round, rosy and chubby cheeks.

The jolly-looking man plays the harmonica with ease, all his movements are soft and paused. His delight is palpable; He's transfixed seemingly basking in joy.

His eyes are closed, his eyelids relaxed. Even his breathing is relaxed; as if assuaged by his own melody.

Totally comfortable he barely blows or inhales into the instrument. "Have a seat young lady," the jolly-looking man says pointing at a grassy clearing in front of him.

Still, without opening his eyes he continues to play, Sofia hesitates at first but cautiously does as told.
"Are you enjoying the forest?"
"Kind of..."
"Why a half-hearted answer?"
Sofia is startled, the jolly-looking man has stopped playing, yet the music tune continues.

"A few things that bother me about the past," pensive she replies.
"Are you referring to matters that no longer exist?"
"Yes," she says defensively, bothered, she asks, "excuse me, why do you keep your eyes closed...oh...are you?"

"Blind, yes I am, but only through my eyes."

Embarrassed, Sofia struggles with what to do or say next.

"Are those memories poisoned with anger and resentment?"

The jolly-looking man asks. "Yes."

"So, you are using and wasting your valuable time on planet earth on the negative side of your past?"

Sofia nods in confirmation.

"Well, grudges are thieves."

"Thieves?"

"Yes! They happily steal life's time from you."

"Happily?"

"Oh yes. Happily, because you let them do so. In fact, you place and keep them inside of you. In fact, you are their host. And a very good one indeed. Naturally, your grudges don't want to leave you. They know they are welcomed guests within your tortured mind and spirit."

"Well jolly-looking man, fact is; they control me I can't get rid of them!" She says protesting.

"Let's face it Sofia, it is you who doesn't want to get rid of them."

"No, that's not true...wait a minute, how do you know my name?"

"Young Seamstress, I told you already; I see and sense people and things without the use or need of my eyesight."

The young seamstress' attention level raises even more.

"The first thing you need to understand is that whatever affected you in the past, way back then, no longer exists. It only resides in your mind and imagination," the jolly-looking man says.

"I think about what I resent all the time,"

"That's another reason holding grudges is a foolish game; how senseless is to repeat the same movie over and over again in your mind. Besides, think about this: Grudging makes you think or wish ill for others but the one poisoned with anger is you."

"How do I uninvite this pack of thieves?"

"Beginning by being happy, valuing and appreciating who you are, what you have whatever that is, but never, ever with what you are not, don't have, much less with what you pretend to be. Many times, we are angry at others because deep inside we see or perceive them as better than us."

"At present, I don't do either of those two things that well."

"Finally, stop judging others and use that energy and time to judge yourself first. That way you constantly keep an eye on your life and actions, propitiating growth and change within you."

"Thank you very much, jolly-looking man. This is a life lesson that I will treasure forever," Sofia says.

The Seamstress waving good-bye strolls back through the forest humming along with the same melody that continues to spread all around her.

The jolly-looking man continues to play incessantly.

On the other hand, the young seamstress laughs in joy, finally freed from grudges -those poisonous thieves- forever.

"Grit"

Grit provides "lasting" quality to endurance and resilience.

Grit is that unbreakable resolve,
driven passion,
resolute behavior,
unstoppable intensity,
overwhelming fortitude,
perennial discipline,
indomitable courage,
tenacious firmness
and unbreakable resolve,
that turns us into deliberate super-achievers,
and perennially likely winners.

Grit is,
where the edginess of a driven character, resides.

Grit is,
where unyielding determination to withstand fear, fatigue,
privation, sickness, endless repetition, failure, rejection, sickness,
tragedy, and pain, lies.

"Perseverance"

The sustained action regardless of circumstances,
the continued pursuit and advancement until completion
are the trademarks of the perseverant person.

Perseverance is indefectible persistence,
unrelenting steadfastness,
immutable continuance,
perennial diligence,
indefatigable stamina,
stubborn doggedness,
and obstinate insistence.

The perseverant person never deviates from their plan,
course of action, or goals;
never tires,
abandons, or quits;
overcomes every obstacle,
always gets back-up
and infallibly gets the job done.

"The Greatest Journeyman that ever Lived"

The rumor has spread all over Venice. The great journeyman is coming back home. An immense crowd has gathered at the San Marco square waterfront. Finally, the merchant ship coming from Constantinople makes its entrance and docks. A plank is immediately extended. Soon, a Burly man with a red long beard with little quick hops crosses the wooden platform and touches the ground in his birthplace and hometown for the first time in 25 years. Numerous relatives of him have gathered among the crowd.

"Venice at last!" He declares.

"Oh my god it is you! You've grown into a man," says one of his aunts with a proud voice.
"We thought you were dead, Marco," says an aunt overcome by emotion.
"That's what I thought on many occasions as well,"

Marco Polo walks surrounded by family and friends. He contemplates the familiar sight and feels immediately at home.
"Nothing has changed," he says with a thunderous voice.

"Much has changed Marco Polo, our current rulers don't like Venetians. But tell me, you must now be a very wealthy man?" asks an uncle.
"In knowledge and experience yes. But I've nothing else to account for. We were robbed in Trebizond of everything we earned and saved through the years."
"It means that you've come back home a poor man?"

"To the contrary, I am a very wealthy man," Marco Polo affirms.

"How Come? Explain yourself," Presses an uncle.

"I have vast faith, knowledge, and experience. Those are the only true components of non-material wealth."

59

"But without riches, you won't be able to acquire a comfortable life, clothes, or other amenities."

"Of course, I will because my faith, knowledge, and experience will open the doors to all of it."

"Didn't you encounter many dangerous situations?"

"Countless. The Tatars do not like merchants, so our encounters with them were always dangerous. Also, at the court of the Emperor of Mongolia, Kublai Khan -whom I served for decades- there were many powerful members of his inner circle that didn't like foreigners like us."

"Marco Polo how were you able to make it through such a long journey?"

"Through Perseverance and Grit,"

"Tell us what each one of those words means to you please,"

"Perseverance is how we continued forward despite difficulties and seemingly insurmountable obstacles. The thought of not completing the journey never crossed our minds. Our grit was the strength of our resolve and determination to reach our destination and complete our mission. Only when we arrived back home moments ago, our journey became successful."

"If you were serving a powerful Emperor, how did he let you come back to Venice?"

"Because he concluded that I was the only person he could trust to deliver a Princess to Persia."

"And did you?"

"Yes, I did. Once my mission was accomplished, I headed home."

"Have you written any diaries about your travels?"

"Whatever I had was lost along the way especially when we were robbed. I intend though to find a writer to whom I will narrate the entire experience."

"Your journey will be remembered as a great adventure."

"Indeed it will. In a way what I did is no different than life itself. We are all embarked on the journey of life. Yet in order to succeed and be happy we always have to keep our goals in mind and always complete our mission. In order to do it, two of the most crucial components are perseverance and grit."

"The 4 Orphan Girls from Vietnam"

The four girls from Ho-Chi-Minh City grew up in a shelter, a place modest but at the same time clean, strict, and filled with love and attention, in other words, a heaven for children without a home.

The childhood friends played, ate, and slept together ever since they could remember, and they attended class at the same public school six days of the week.
Their walks to class were memorable every day.
Holding hands, shouldering their backpacks they ran into numerous children not as lucky as them.

Some looked hungry, and they shared their snacks with them; others seemed lost with their ragged clothes and broken sandals; to those they brought loose clothesthey found at the shelter.

Already 12 Hahn was the oldest among the foursome, by two years.

In the cold winter nights of the rainy season the 4 of them cuddled together in bed to feel warm.

Hahn loved to read to them until the younger 3 fell asleep.

Through countless children's books, the Vietnamese war orphans dreamed about faraway places, fairy tales, fairy godmothers princes in white horses and happy endings.

One good day Hahn made like she was reading but in reality, she was reciting a tale she'd written earlier for her three friends.

There was an important reason why she did so; an important secret only Hahn knew. So, the tale she narrated that day contained a hidden message for her three childhood friends to uncover something Hahn wanted them to never forget.

The story Hanh wrote and recited that night was about a shipwreck on a remote and barren island of the pacific.
After a few weeks, the captain and his crew were starving and hopeless as their location was so remote that not a single ship had crossed the horizon since their arrival.

The captain decided to risk it all and on one of the 2 lifeboats they had been able to save, with the help of his crew, built a small mast and fit a small sail to it sewed with by the vessel's handyman.

With some of the food that was left and water collected from the rainy days, the captain and one crew member set sail into the vast Pacific Ocean.

All his intended destinations were more than 1000 nautical miles away. Before leaving he made a promise to his crew, "I will come back to rescue you all."

The captain and his single mate navigated for 6 weeks, they plowed through calm and heavy seas some were scorching-hot dry days others were plagued with never-ending storms.

When the captain reached land, he worked feverishly to secure his crew's rescue, even though it took him a long time he never stopped until he found a boat to go for his crew.

Almost three months later, when they had almost given up thinking that their captain had either perished or simply saved himself and had forgotten about them, right in the middle horizon the crew saw a vessel arrive.

Soon they saw a tender approach with their captain aboard waving at them. He had never forgotten them; Loyalty to his crew was as strong and theirs to him. He had come to rescue them.

When Hahn finished reciting the story, her three friends were all still awake with big wide and intense eyes of wonder looking at her, cuddled together they fell asleep one more time, wearing placid and happy faces.

The next morning when the three younger Vietnamese girls woke up, Hahn was no longer there.

Their initial surprise and sadness only grew when the orphanage director informed them that Hahn had been adopted by a Japanese couple from the city of Nagoya.

The pensive threesome headed to school that morning in a somber and sad mood. This until they suddenly looked at each other, all thinking exactly the same.

"She will come back for us," they said in tandem with big broad smiles.

How naive their thought, If they only knew.
How could a 12-year-old afford to come to their rescue?

Months passed and Hahn letters started to arrive.

She was enjoying a very nice life with their adoptive parents.
She had picked up the Japanese language in no time.

At school, she was excelling and was enrolled in the gifted program.
Her three friends wondered if with so much happiness and wealth Hanh will end up forgetting them.

More months passed, as Hahn letters described one success after another, a growing feeling of lost hope kept creeping on the 3 young Vietnamese girls.
"Maybe she's not coming back for us after all," they would comment.

But the story of the captain and the rescue of his crew always prevailed in the end…
"She will. There's no doubt. She will come back for us."
Then one good morning as the three girls walked to class a shiny black limousine drove next to them.

Surprised they turned as one of the dark tinted window glasses was lowered. Caught totally by surprise, the three young girls covered their faces, they were at a loss for words, filled with emotion, they jumped up and down seeing their childhood friend back.

"I told you that I was going to come back for you," Hanh said with a voice filled with joy.

The door of the limousine opened, and their older friend jumped and ran towards them. They embraced, hugged, kissed, yelled, and screamed in a state of exuberant happiness. They did so seemingly forever.

The foursome was back together once more.

"How did you do it?" one of her three childhood friends asked,
"Ever since my arrival I worked non-stop to get all you adopted as well. I earned it through my school performance and being such a good daughter that I convinced my adoptive parents -now yours- how hard-working and talented Vietnamese girls are."

"The Young Soprano from the Mountains of Merida"

The Young Soprano's voice is the voice of an angel.

When she sings at the foothills of the "Los Andes" mountain range, the little birds around her sing as well; mimicking her tune, her melody, they form an impromptu chorus filled with the sounds of nature, made right out in Heaven.

When the young Soprano sings the mountain flowers bloom in happiness. The skies become bluer, clearer and the clouds part ways in joy serving as the amphitheater of nature further enhancing the acoustics of her splendorous voice.

When the Young Soprano's voice is heard the waterfalls, creeks, rivers, and lakes celebrate as their trickles, roars, and splashes display crispier, more harmonic and crystalline sounds that further enhance the improvised nature's orchestra.

The Young Soprano's talents is her ticket to the National Academy of Music in the capital city of Caracas. Very few make it into the famous school, but she is surely meant to be one of them.

For weeks, months, and years the Young Soprano studies, trains and prepares, working day and night, harder than most, more than anyone. Her life-long mentor, with long white braids, a benign face, and a former Soprano herself, gently guides the Young Soprano as she grows and becomes a better and better performer.

Best of all, the knowledgeable tutor knows the young Soprano better than anyone else, even herself. In the days where dark clouds obscure the spirit and render inutile the immense talent of the Young Soprano, the stern hand of her middle-aged mentor quickly restores reality and pulls the advantaged singer out of the dark holes she sometimes tends to fall or place herself on.

"What troubles you today, Isabella?" Asks Theresa, her mentor.

"I have difficulty trusting anyone," The young Soprano responds.

"I know dear. I know. But what about me, don't you trust me?"

"I guess I do."

"Why the hesitation?"

"No, no, sorry. Of course I do."

"Isabella, your mom's sudden illness and unintended departure is nobody's fault and most certainly not hers."

"But she left me all alone."

"You are not alone. You've never been alone. Your father's life is centered around you. He loves you to no end. Additionally, you have all your mother's sisters -your aunts- always doting on you unlimited love and affection. You also have me guiding your prodigious talent and you have the gift of your mother's voice."

"I get all of that but sometimes I feel angry and abandoned."

"You have to fight those feelings. I am sure that your mom is up there in Heaven, immensely proud of all your accomplishments."

One good day, the anticipated letter finally arrives. Isabella has been invited by the National Academy Of Music for an interview and test to consider her admission to the prestigious school.

"Theresa, Theresa!" She yells while entering her mentor's school office.

The place is empty. She goes to her classroom, but she isn't there either. Finally, Isabella runs to the gardens where her gentle mentor sometimes goes for a stroll. No luck either.

"Where's she?" she mulls while walking back to school.

"Isabella, there you are. I was looking for you all over the place," says the school principal, Mrs. Gutierrez.

"I've been running around looking for Mrs. Theresa."

"That's precisely what I wanted to talk to you about."

Isabella looks at the school principal with alarm and anxiety in her eyes.

"She was taken to the hospital an hour ago."

"What happened to her? Is she alright?"

"She's sick Isabella. She wants to talk to you, go and visit her right away."

Isabella walks and runs to the only hospital in town. Her face is inundated with tears; Her entire self is saturated with fear. When she reaches the door of her mentor's hospital room, the knot on her throat grows by the minute. The first sight of the weakened and pale image of her tutor leaves the Young Soprano speechless and in shock.

"Isabella dear, it is so nice for you to come,"

"Came the moment I heard, Mrs. Theresa."

"Dear, I've not been doing well for a while. I'd hoped to get better and spare the worry to all, especially you. But things have not turned out the way I expected."

"Mrs. Theresa you are not going to…? Are you going to leave me? you can't!" says Isabella crying and sobbing.

"Come here my love. Come," Theresa says.

Hesitantly, Isabella approaches her convalescent mentor.
They embrace and hug seemingly forever.

"Isabella, I want you to promise me that you will go to Caracas, have a wonderful interview and secure your entry into the National School of Music."

"No!"

"Why?"

"Without you, I can't do it. It's over. My life's over."

Shaking her head in refusal, Isabella stands with her arms crossed and an awfully contorted face. That is when she sees her mentor cry profusely. It's a cry filled with pain, and it jolts the Young and

Talented Soprano to the core. That's the catalyst that makes her snap back to reality. The Young Soprano approaches her mentor once more. The hug that follows is warm and comforting.

"Of course I will, Mrs. Theresa. Please forgive me. It was just a tantrum of mine."
"Oh Isabella, you have no idea how happy you make me. Though you still have to work hard in overcoming the trauma of the loss of your mother."
"I promise I will, Mrs. Theresa."
"Well, let's get down to work then. I have to prepare you for the interview. I also have to write a detailed letter of recommendation for you. Without it, it is unlikely that they'll admit you."

For several days straight, they work together at the Young Soprano's mentor's hospital room. They toil for hours and hours at a time, until Mrs. Theresa deems her mentee ready.

"Dear, Tomorrow we will rehearse one more time and you should be good to go after that."

But those are the last words the young Soprano ever hears again from her beloved mentor. The next day when she shows up at the hospital, she's said that her mentor passed away the night before.
At a loss at first, then utterly angry, the young Soprano turns around and heads home, where she locks herself up in her room. And does not leave for days. She even stops singing and vows to never do it again.

Finally, her father knocks at her door.
"Isabella, I'm heading to your mentor's funeral. You have to show yourself up over there and pay your respects. Mrs. Theresa gave so much of herself to you. You owe it to her."
"I'm not going!"
Nelson, her father enters the room and faces his daughter with a stern face. "Why on earth will you do that?"

"She failed me."

"How can you say that?"

"She abandoned me."

"No. She didn't. She was very ill and passed away. She didn't want to leave you. God took her away dear," he says while hugging Isabella.

"Yes, she did. Exactly like mom did," Isabella says aloud as she begins to cry inconsolably.

"Why don't you change, we have to get going," her father says stepping outside.

Without uttering a word, Isabella does as tell.

Minutes later they head together to the funeral. At the funeral, her deceased mentor's own daughter, Megan, approaches the young Soprano.

"Isabella, just moments before she passed away, my mom asked me to pass along a message,"

Puzzled, Isabel listens attentively.

"She said: Tell Isabella not to forget the promise she made to me."

Isabella gives Megan a half-smile of respect while she drags her father out and leaves in a hurry.

"Isabella, the interview is the day after tomorrow,"

"Father, I want to go but is pointless."

"Why?"

"My tutor betrayed..."

"What kind of a word is that, Isabella!" Nelson says interrupting her in disgust.

At that moment Isabella finally realizes that she's been accusing and blaming her loved ones for the pain of losing them.

"I'm sorry dad. Of course she didn't betray me. Mom didn't betray me either. That's wrong for me to say. The reason I won't go is because Mrs. Theresa couldn't get to write a letter of recommendation for the National Academy of Music. Without it, is unlikely that I will be accepted."

"I see. So what are you going to do about it? Simply give up and quit?"

Isabella feels liberated as if an unbearable and heavy weight has been lifted from her shoulders.
"Tell you what dad. I will nevertheless go and give it my best shot. Truth be told, Mrs. Theresa prepared me well for it."

Isabella's interview takes place soon after and she succeeds in every category with flying colors. The rehearsals of her voice go even better. The moment of truth arrives when she completes the last exerting evaluation; before leaving she addresses the acceptance committee, one more time.

"Thank you for your interest in me. I want you to know that I am aware that without my mentor's letter of recommendation I won't be accepted. I understand this and accept it. But next year, you can rest assured that I will try again." She says to the Admissions Committee.

She is ready to go back home, a bit sad but mainly satisfied that she did her best.

"Young Soprano, what makes you believe that you won't be accepted?" One of the members of the committee asks.

"Don't take it as an excuse but my tutor passed away before she could write the letter of recommendation you require. I came nevertheless to honor a promise I made to her."

"You came just to fulfill a promise?"

Isabella thinks long and hard. She stares with intense eyes at her examiners. Then decides to blurt the truth the way she feels it.
"Also, because I feel that I am ready for it."

"Ready for what if I may ask?" Asks another member of the admissions committee.

"Ready to be admitted in the Academy and not only succeed but also be one of its top performers."

"Isabella. First of all, your mentor did send to us a detailed letter of recommendation about you weeks ago." Says a lady member of the committee.

Emotions build up in a hurry in Isabella's chest, her lower lip trembles, a couple of teardrops slowly slide through her cheeks.

"Second, we would have accepted you anyhow without it. That's how well prepared and talented you are."

Isabella jumps in joy and hugs her father. She politely shakes hands with every member saying thank you to each one of them.

She then walks out proudly holding her father's arm.
"And Isabella...," says the same lady member,

The young Soprano turns around, "Yes?"

"Your mentor also said in her letter that if you showed up and a scene like this ever happened, to tell you to look in your assignments folder."

Isabella quickly opens the folder she hasn't opened for weeks.
Page after page she contemplates the impeccable work of her mentor until at the very back of the folder she sees the envelope.

"Letter of Recommendation for the National Academy of Music." It was always there! She realizes.

When she opens it, she finds a little note with the letter,
"Worse than betrayal is to falsely accuse our loved ones of such an offense."

"The Ace Pilots encounter in the deep ends of the Rain Forest"
(Amazonia 1960s.)

"Many, many years ago, I met in the jungle an extraordinary man that became my best friend in life. But things did not start well at all when we first met each other," says the old man as he narrates for the first time to his grandson one of the key moments of his life.

"Grandpa, is this another one of those war stories of yours?"
Asks his grandson with big wide eyes and a voice filled with excitement.

"Yes and no. Be a little bit patient and you'll see," says the many times decorated war hero.

The excited grandchild cuddles closer to his grandfather on the reading chair they use every night.
"It starts like this…"

Flying over the Venezuelan plains, the battered twin engine is facing in the distance the vast Amazon rainforest. Straight ahead a wall of dense nature, splashed with endless shades of green, lazily draws nearer and nearer.

Once more the mysterious and untamed jungle awaits the arrival of Samuel Ely Saperstein an experienced World War II American pilot. After flying in and out of the remote region over the last two decades, he feels as comfortable with the familiar surroundings as with the humming of the sputtering engines, and the sight of the peeling paint of his dependable Piper Aztec.

At first, they seem like tiny obelisks far ahead. As he flies closer, they seem like a formation of giant totems protuberating above the treetops in the horizon.
He can now see clearly the peculiar flat-top, vertically-narrow,

pre-historical mountains called -Tepuis - by the locals.

The ace pilot initiates the preparations to execute the harrowing, dare-devil landing. One he's performed hundreds of times before.

Saperstein descends to one thousand feet pointing the aircraft to the clearing lying atop a gigantic Tepui in the middle of the rainforest.
As usual, he makes his first pass above the site with his engines at full throttle. The frequent visitor wants the unmistakable noise to be noticed.

As he banks and turns back in the distance, machetes on hand, countless Yaomani Indians emerge from the jungle and run towards the clearing. Frantically, they all start chopping away the waist-high brush and foliage.

As the familiar plane makes a second pass, the Yaomani wave at their trusted provider of vital supplies including medicines and essential tools like their priced machetes.

Moments later, after a deft, precision landing executed with only a couple of bounces within a couple of hundred yards, the plane comes to a stand-still.

The tribe's leader, Itakere greets Saperstein right after he jumps off the aircraft.
The long-time friends embrace while the plane is off-loaded.

"Welcome back old friend," says Itakere in perfect English.
"Glad to be here." Says the pilot.
"There's much to talk about," the tribe's leader says.
"Certainly. Looking forward. here are your books." The airman says.
"Always an honor. Your generous heart has helped me build a precious book collection," The head tribe's man says.

74

"Always a pleasure," The pilot says.
"But before we get started there's someone I want you to meet."

At the tribe's fire pit a bearded man lies, he looks sick and emaciated; several bandages cover his extremities as well.

"He flies planes and is also a World War II pilot like you. Nowadays, he's a river pilot," the tribe's leader says. "We rescued him days ago down the Orinoco a half a day's walk from here."

Samuel's eyes grow wide with interest.

"Did he crash?"
"Yes, A floating plane into the river; That is why he is still alive. Because he hit the water instead of land or trees."

Hours later as they play one of their memorable chess matches, the injured man wakes up. His seems dazed and struggles to regain focus.

When he finally sees the American Pilot his eyes first grow wide in total surprise, then relaxed at the sight of another jungle visitor like him.

The two players take notice and turn their attention to the river pilot.

The American pilot stands up and approaches the convalescent man.
"Samuel Ely Saperstein," he says extending his hand.
"Ernesto Otto Gerlach," The injured pilot responds extending his.

As they shake hands, the heavy German accent is immediately recognized by Saperstein. He immediately drops Gerlach's hand, turns on his heels, and walks away, without uttering a single additional word. The tribe's leader is caught by surprise as much as Gerlach does.

'Mr. Gerlach let go and find out what's just happened in here. I'll be right back."

Itakere finds Samuel pacing back and forth inside his habitual sleeping quarters. When the tribesman approaches, Samuel waves his hand at him in a gesture that means both that he doesn't want to talk and wants to be left alone.

Itakere returns pensive to the fire pit and the convalescent pilot. But when he takes a look at the wounded man lying in the floor, a bit obfuscated, he decides to go back a have a word with his old friend.

"Do you guys know each other? Is there a problem between the two of you?"
"No, I've never met him before."
"Why your reaction then?"
"He's a German and I'm a Jew, you wouldn't understand."
"Of course I do, not only because your books have educated me about what happened in World War II but also because of your attitude is no different than the behavior that some warring factions have against each other over here in the jungle."

The tribe's man approaches his old friend and places an arm around him.
"C'mon follow me, let's go and talk to your fellow airman."

At the fire pit they find the wounded German Pilot sitting straight with a still startled face. Both men contemplate each other for a long time. This until Samuel lets it go.

"All my uncles, aunts, cousins, nieces, grandparents and childhood friends died in concentration camps at the hands of you Nazis," says panting the American Jewish pilot,

"The only reason my parents -rip- my siblings and I survived the war is because we'd moved to America before the war started, this because my father was hired away by an American University," adds Samuel,

"So, as a teenager I enlisted myself and went to fight you guys as soon I was old enough and I did it in the sky downing as many of your planes as humanly and physically possible," continues Samuel.

An uneasy silence follows as the German pilot listens to every word being said. His demeanor is natural, his face does not show discomfort much less guilt. With profound warmth in his voice, he replies…

"I don't know anything about you, Sir but I feel your profound pain and sorrow. First of all, I was never a Nazi; and don't take this as me repeating the typical, uncomfortable but convenient excuse still overheard in Germany decades after the war, even today, repeated by many who don't really believe or feel that way. No, in my case I wasn't born in Germany but in this beautiful South-American country of Venezuela, in the oil region of Zulia. When I was 12 years old my German-born parents sent me to Hamburg to complete my high school in Germany. They wanted me to get acquainted with our relatives, as well as the country's culture. Over there I discovered my passion for flying, so, at 14 I started to fly gliders. Unfortunately, at 16 I was forcefully recruited to the German air force -The Luftwaffe- towards the end of the war they were running out of everything including pilots, so teenage boys like me were sent to war. I only lasted six months flying for them; on a reconnaissance mission, I was shot down over Poland and was captured the moment I touched ground with my parachute and became a prisoner of war. Although the war ended shortly thereafter, I spent two years at a concentration camp. I was released only because suffering pneumonia they thought I was dying. With a fellow prisoner equally sick as myself, we started to walk, as both of us were half-naked wearing only a pair of shorts; on the first Polish village they gave us shirts and sandals. We walked all the way to Hamburg. I found a city totally destroyed and my relatives in disarray. The only thing I wanted was to return to my home country. And I did, but not before procuring myself with travel documents. In order to do that I had to traverse and hitchhike going south across a devastated and hungry Germany all the way to Bern in Switzerland where at the Venezuelan embassy I could finally get a passport. Then I had to traverse the whole of Germany again, this time going north until Oslo, Norway; the only place where cargo ships were heading to Venezuela. After three months wait, I finally was able to get into a ship and made my way over here and that was forty and some years ago. But I never stopped flying and the Amazon has been my home for many years now," says the German-Venezuelan pilot.

Samuel's tears inundate his face.

"I am so, so, sorry, please forgive me," he says.
"There is nothing to forgive, as you can see, I have no feelings of guilt about World War II. I am ashamed for what Germany did, but I wasn't part of it, at least not voluntarily. And the same goes as well for the vast majority of Germans today -especially 40 plus years later-. Sir, although you can and shall never forget, you have to learn to forgive them but especially yourself," Concludes the German-Venezuelan ace pilot.

The next day, with profound satisfaction and proud of his old friend Itakere sees him leaving. Doing the dutiful with gusto with the help of the tribesman, Samuel loads the wounded German-Venezuelan pilot into his plane. From atop a Tepui -the house of the gods- in the local language, Samuel throttles his 2 propellers at full power for the narrowing and short take-off. And once more from the improvised runaway on the flattop prehistoric mountain,

78

the plane barely lifts off, brushing the top of the trees at the end of the runway, on the way up.

From then on, the couple of sixty-plus-year-olds establish a long-lasting friendship; One a German-Venezuelan ace pilot the other an American Jewish flying ace himself. an unbreakable bond that is to last to the end of their lives.

"Not Everything We Hear is What Appears to Be"

Falsehoods can be deceiving,
and although they reside
on the other side of reality's spectrum,
truisms can be elusive as well.

Often, we don't mean what we say,
this occurs when what we really think or do
is not in sync with what comes out of our mouths.

When in private we deviate
from what we really want
not only are we not pursuing the truth,
we are also attempting to create a false reality
where we may end up believing our own lies.

Hence detecting false negatives or false positives
becomes an existential imperative.

What we hear, what is said,
Suddenly loses weight, value, and respect.

What matters then
is what was really meant
with words we heard
as not everything we hear
is what appears to be,
but something else.

"The Luthier from Mittenwald"

In the realm of Violins, Violas, and Cellos, there was once an art-crafter extraordinaire -A Luthier- to whom there was no equal in the whole wide world.

His name was Leo Schoeffer.
He was born in a small town called Mittenwald in the region of Bavaria, Southern Germany.
His tinkering skills went way beyond crafting, repairing, restoring, fine-tuning even stringing any of those precious instruments.

His incomparable abilities were not only in the quality of his work neither on his level of craftsmanship when working the wood - which were both better to none- what distinguished him as the best Luthier, there ever was, was the fact that Leo could "feel" and "breath" the string instruments as well.

One splendorous winter night, while attending a concert gala in Munich, the largest city of Bavaria; The Luthier observed attentively that within the beauty and magnificence of the music performance, although not noticeable to the audience, his trained eyes and ears detected that something was amiss with the leading Violinist.

This anomaly was taking place in spite that all that could be heard throughout the concert hall, was the crispiness of glorious, masterful music; It was the sound of Heaven and Angels.

And yet to the experienced Luthier the intimate and profound connection between the Violinist and his instrument, were simply not there.

After an "Apotheosical" grand finale, the Fiddler and the Philharmonic Orchestra were acclaimed at length by the public;

81

three times the curtain dropped, three times it had to be raised to the continued applause; Shortly after, the ever-perceptive Luthier went backstage to meet his longtime client, the leading Violinist.

"What's wrong?" Asked the Luthier.
"I don't know, is a mystery to me," Replied the Fiddler.
"Did you drop it?"
"No"
"Did you hit something with it?"
"Neither. As usual, it never leaves my eyesight until safely stored away at home."
"Tuning, perhaps?"
"Either. It's perfectly tuned."
"Let me take a look."

With great care the Violinist handed the centuries-old Stradivarius, worth millions, to the only person in the world, other than him, allowed to touch his most irreplaceable instrument.

First, with deliberate pause, The Luthier drew the violin close to his ear while gently knocking -using a single knuckle- every inch of the wooden surface.
He carefully listened to the echoes' acoustics, resonating throughout the violin's inner chamber.

Next, using them as the palm of a hand, he proceeded to delicately slide three fingers over the violin's carcass, feeling every curve, angle, and joint of the invaluable musical instrument; He did this with his eyes closed, seeking and expecting absolute perfection and smoothness in the old masterfully crafted wood.

When finished, The Luthier smiled at the Fiddler.

"Let me work at it. I'll find out what's happening."

The next day,

The Luthier returned the Stradivarius to the Violinist.

"Play it, please," The Craftsman asked.

The eager artist, fiddle-bow on his right hand, his violin over his extended left arm; quickly mounted the violin on his shoulder and against his chin. But just before the virtuoso started to play, The Luthier noticed the discomfort on the genial artist, once more. Sure enough, the moment the musician rendered a couple of notes with his beloved instrument; He stopped.

"Still the same problem. What's wrong?" Said the frustrated Violinist.

With a benign smile, The Luthier approached the Fiddler.

"Don't move the instrument," The Luthier said.

With great care and deft touch, The Luthier ever so slightly moved the position of the violin on The Violinist's shoulder.

"Now place your chin back on it,"

The Luthier asked.
The Fiddler did and his face was immediately illuminated.

Totally transformed, he unleashed a 10 minutes solo, releasing all of his repressed musical passion and desire with fury and joy.

"What did you do to it?"

An exhausted yet beaming Fiddler said.
"Frankly speaking…nothing…" The Luthier responded.

The Violinist reacted with total surprise.
"But I still earned my fee though…

"You see, I spent hours evaluating your Stradivarius; Besides minute tinkering, nothing else was necessary. I concluded that the issue was of a different kind. So, I went back in my mind to your concert performance and your subtle discomfort," explained The Luthier.

"You noticed it?" Asked a startled Fiddler.
"Of course, I did, I know your routine quite well by now."
"How did you fix…?"

The Violinist began to say but interrupted himself.

"My posture?" He asked.
"Not exactly. It was all in the positioning of your Stradivarius on your shoulder. When I went back in my mind to the concert I replayed your performance over and over again, until I noticed the subtle change compared to the past."
"One tiny tad, and you noticed it?" The Violinist asked.
"That's right, the apparent mechanical correction placed you in the right frame of mind to cause the imperative symbiosis and communion, the ONENESS between the violin and you," The Luthier said…Then added, "In people like you that's the only way how the superb, incomparable quality of your Stradivarius violin and your immense talents come out simultaneously and in full display. An ever so diminutive deviation, just a tad, is the difference between ordinary Greatness and utter, unfettered and galloping Genius," concluded the masterful art-crafter.

"The Young Girl from Budapest"

The young girl walked the ruined streets of Budapest, her ragged clothes and worn-out shoes matched the hungry look and sad eyes drawn on her face. A loaf of bread here, a cup of warm soup there, were handouts barely enough to sustain her, but not for much longer.

There was nothing left of the home where she was born, just rubbles and debris, where the magnificent residence once was. She had no idea if any member of her family was still alive, four years earlier she had been sent to a convent high up in the Italian Dolomite Mountains in care and protection of her aunt, her mother's sister, the nun.

"Sophia, the war may soon reach Budapest, you'll be safe with Clara," said her mother. Your brother will be staying with your uncle Alfonzo in New York," her mom added referring to her father's brother.

"And the two of you? Why are you staying? Why aren't we all leaving together?" asked Sophia.

"Because we have to protect our home and your father's factory," her mother said. "Besides, this may all soon be over, in that case, we will bring you back right away,"

"I want all of us to stay together here at home, mom."

"I am sorry Sophia but it is not safe at the moment for you to be here," her mother said with finality.

Early the next morning Sophia was sent by train to the convent in the high mountains of Italy. But not before a somber and tearful farewell took place. Her parents and her younger brother Thomaz waving goodbye were the last images she had of them.

All she knew was that soon after she arrived at the convent, Budapest had been taken over by the Nazis. She didn't even know if her brother had made it to America or not. None of her letters to Budapest and the U.S. were ever replied to.

Four years later, the war just over; Already 18 years old, a young adult; Sophia decided to go back home against the strong wishes of her aunt, the nun.

Now, finally back in her hometown, she didn't know what to do, nor did she have any place to go. She sat for hours at the doorstep of her house, the only thing left standing in the property. She cried softly, her sobs coming and going as waves of sadness and longing inundated her. First, they came to her like a whisper. She tried to focus and get out of the haze she was in.

"Sophie is that you?" were the faint words she now heard.

Slowly, she lifted her head as if hypnotized. The sight of her parents and her now grown-up sibling did not register as first. In a haze and fainting, she thought she was hallucinating as the three figures moved in slow motion towards her, which in reality was literally running. She finally reacted in a snap. Her eyes expanded, her stare filled with primal intensity.

"Mother, Father, Thomaz," she yelled.

Her lips trembling and her heart pounding, Sophia jumped then ran with whatever energy she had left; They all hugged and kissed to no end, the whole family was all together again.

"We went to pick you up at the convent, your aunt told us you were on your way over here. We know you were all safe but had a hard time," said her mom.
"We were incommunicado from the world mother. During the last few months there was hardly any food, coal, or wood," said Sophie.
"We didn't fare much better either. Hiding in a monastery high up on the Tatra mountains of Slovakia. We lost everything, Sophie," said her father.
"No, we didn't, we have it all, dad. We have everything. We have us!" said the young girl from Budapest.

"Together, As Ever, As One"

We are all on this together,

we are as ever one.

Make it we are going to,

physically distant

but closer than ever before.

We are going to make it through,

Together, as ever, as one.

It silently spreads...

ruthlessly attempting

to undermine our Society,

threatening the way we live as we know it,

all at once.

There is only one problem,

for the virus to win,

and that is US!

It has to knock us down first,

but that can't or won't happen,

It is not even an option!

Because of You, Me, He, She, Them.

Because of all of us!

Stubbornly through great sacrifices,

resilient and enduring,

we are simply not letting the disease

exponentially grow around us.

You see...

Besides Your and our Sacrifices,

as importantly…

Some of us do miracles by the minute,

Some of us are fearless warriors,

relentlessly attacking head-on

an insidious enemy.

Our unsung HEROES,

We Honor and Salute You,

We are forever Grateful,

We are forever Humbled,

We are forever Inspired

by You!

You are all,

EVERYWHERE you need to be,

ANYWHERE you are required to be,

FOR AS LONG AS is needed to be,

You are always WHERE you must be.

Laboring through the day,

Laboring through the night,

We all depend on you,

and do so with our eyes closed,

trusting without restrain and blind faith.

Incessantly putting yourselves in harm's way,

sacrificing it all for the common good,

you lose some but save many and much more.

You also light and lead the way for us all,

through this biological storm,

for our indomitable herd to conquer the disease,

stopping nature right on its tracks.

You Bring Grandma Back to Life,

You Preserve Grandpa for us to enjoy,

You Rescue and Save:

our Moms and Dads,

our Sons and Daughters,

our Aunties and Uncles,

Our Nieces and Nephews,

Cousins, Friends, and Neighbors;

You Gift us back Anyone and Everyone

from the Jaws of Death.

As we Fight and Fight,

Toil and Toil,

pushing back,

laboring without respite to defeat the virus,

not letting it grow.

We defend the Human Race

with a single goal in mind,

To Never Ever,

Never, Ever, Ever,

Give-Up

on this precious Life we all enjoy.

It silently spreads…

trying to undermine our Society,

But it won't win!

It has to knock us down first,

but that can't happen.

It is not even an option,

simply because

We won't let it happen,

We won't let it be!

This abominable infection

is in actuality

an existential opportunity,

where,

We Love and Care,

We are Gentle and Kind,

We Feel and Share,

We Give Without Asking,

We enjoy each other's company like never before,

We communicate and play better than ever before,

And suddenly,

We are infinitely more appreciative

of Everyone and Everything around us.

Additionally,

We learn and then some

about ourselves and each other,

especially about:

Closeness,

Intimacy,

Empathy,

The Importance of the Small Details in Life

and How to Wake-Up from the "Haze" and "Spoils"

of a "Convenient" and "Comfortable" World,

conquering "Routine," "Boredom" and "Lack of Purpose,"

once for all.

We also make-up for "Lost Time"

and "Time Apart,"

learn how to use it better

and finally, understand

what "Saving for a Rainy Day" means.

Through it all,

We

Revisit,

Reconnect,

Reunite,

Reencounter,

Retrain,

Relearn,

Rethink,

Redo,

Retake,

Reset,

Replant,

Retry, Retry and Retry,

Refine and Reimagine.

In other words,

We acquire the Gift

of Restarting Life all over again.

We are all on this together,

We are going to make it through,

Together, As Ever, as One.

"The Puppet Master and the Inquisitive Youngster"

As the puppet-master pulled the strings with skill and artistry the marionettes made the audience -especially the children- laugh to no end.

In every one of his moves, he remained hidden behind the small boxy stage. Through the puppeteer's vocal talents, the lively, jumpy characters went at each other; arguing, singing, laughing, yelling, cursing, and talking in high -pitched -Falsetto- voices.

Yet in the end, the feisty figures always made up, to the joy and delight of the small crowds that gathered every day to attend the show. The puppet master traveled like a gypsy in a never-ending itinerary presenting his compact spectacle at tiny town squares, through cozy Greek seaside fishing villages, along the Ionic Sea.

The primarily white architecture on the tightly bunched enclaves, contrasted harmonically with a cornucopia of folkloric colors; the verandas, balconies, rooftops, artful pots, sidewalks, and countless flowers painted everything with an air of delightful joy.

All of it is a perfect corollary of friendliness for the puppeteer's act to thrive and resonate with each Mediterranean spot he visited, and the appreciative populace regaled with his show.

One particular afternoon as he winded down the show a youngster waited patiently or the old puppeteer to free himself up.

"Puppeteer, Puppeteer, your show makes me really, really happy," the youngster said as the performer released his props.
"Thank you very much; your words are very kind," the street artist replied.
"Sir, I was wondering how much control you have over your marionettes?"

"That is a very perceptive question you ask, young man. But tell me, what prompts you to quiz me in such manner?"

"Well, it seems to me that although you pull all of their strings for your puppets to come alive; once your deft maneuvering sets them off, they seem to have a life all of their own. Even their voices seem to be beyond you. It is as if while acting, you split into multiple personas, characters, and personalities that takes possession of you."

In the background of the deepening conversation; string instruments and animated Greek dances with even more colorful attires blended with the gentle sea breeze. For what seemed like an eternity the puppeteer observed the youngster with bemused but respectful eyes.

"Let me share with you what goes on behind the scenes... Like in life, deliberately, consciously or not; We, You, Me, Them are always pulling some of the strings."

"But what we seek or aim to control never ever works exactly like we want or expect it to be."

"You are right, sometimes things adopt a life all of their own and that's certainly my case," said the puppeteer.

"Aren't you uncomfortable not to be in control of the show and the strings you pull?" asked the youngster.

"No, I am not that's how everything works and flows in life. we pull them but we are not the strings; we steer and drive them, but we are not the marionettes; we script and rehearse; we fine-tune, correct, and fix them, over and over again, yet we are not the performance or the act itself," reflected the dexterous artist.
Then continued,

"When it's show time, the artist, the creator and the string master in me, all become secondary to the puppets and marionettes; Those unruly, chaotic figures are the ones who go and steal the show," adds the itinerant performer.

"So, it is true then, while in the act the puppets and the marionettes are really alive," the inquisitive youngster said.

"In a sense yes! At least that's the way you perceive it. That's what you believe. Yet, in as much as it seems that a puppet master like me, controls all the strings and marionettes; Like in life, that is only partially true; actually, sometimes I am the puppet or marionette myself; Further, depending on how we look at it, in a way, once the show starts, I hardly have any control, not at least until the very end," the puppet master said.

"And what happens when it's over, are you back in control?" asked the quizzing young man.

"Yes, I am but only of inert and lifeless objects and props; Without the show, the act, the public and the performance, the magic is simply...Gone!" the wise artist said, then added,

"As a puppet master, I exercise control and pull the strings while letting that what I manipulate be their own characters and personas. And that's exactly like it works in life, we don't control anything or anyone but us. We can hardly guide, steer and rehearse the rest. Life is like a puppets and marionettes show with a life all of its own."

"The Troll and The Determined Youngster from Tromso"

The view from high-up at the flat-top bedrock, is stunning, seemingly it goes on for miles and miles to no end; underneath, deep blues and greens can be seen, depicting a perfect Norwegian postcard of immense and sinuous water expanses; filled with jagged bays and estuaries –the famous Nordic fjords– water channels framed by vertical and giant mountains, on both sides saturate it all.

The youngster grew up in the long days and nights of Tromso, located way, way up in the land of Vikings not far from Nordcap, the northern most civilized place in the world before the north pole. Today's effort to reach the top of the mountain is the culmination of a long recovery for young Oleg.

After his third birthday, he was not able to walk, not even move his legs any longer. A bacteria they said, had affected his lower extremities and motor-skills.

He breaths deeply inhaling with pleasure the temperate air of the mountain summit. He stands on both legs, those he was told countless times he was never going to be able to use, ever again.

"So, you finally made it, Young Oleg," says with a thunderous voice the troll of the mountain, his longtime friend.

Short, with a big head and a long-corrugated nose, wearing a coned-floppy cap and "Tyrolean" shorts with suspenders, the mountain troll is never this friendly with anyone. To the contrary, his reputation through a centuries old life is one of mischief, havoc and mayhem.

But his relationship with the determined youngster has been different from the beginning. It all began inauspiciously, a tiny boy of eight perhaps nine years old at the base of the big mountain, choosing not to take the cable car but instead, to hike it up.

The detestable figure contemplated the youngster's feat with disdain and skepticism.
'He could ride the tram for a few minutes and be at the top; this boy is a fool,' reflected the mountain troll while contemplating Young Oleg with leg braces and crutches trying to walk up the mountain.

"Why do you bother? You'll never make it," said the troll while standing atop of a rock with his arms crossed.

The handicapped youngster barely acknowledged his presence.
"I may not make it today, but eventually I will," Oleg said with a big broad smile.

The mountain troll was truly impressed. His mere presence, together with a hideous voice, always intimated others.
But not this youngster.
'Who is he?' An intrigued troll asked himself.

That day Oleg was barely able to walk a few hundred meters.
But the next morning the young boy was at it once more and this time managed twice the distance.

"Why do you torture yourself?" the mountain troll asked.
"I am enjoying the effort Troll, don't you understand?" Oleg said.
"Not really," replied an incredulous Troll.

Throughout the summer Oleg continued to make progress.
Sometimes he didn't advance much in distance or anything at all.
But he compensated with better balance and less effort overall.

What really amazed the mountain troll was that when the long winter nights arrived Oleg did not stop coming and trying to conquer the mountain again and again.

Same time at midday everyday under a tenuous sun, like clockwork he showed up and continued advancing two steps forward, one backwards, three forward…

"What do you want out of this?" the mountain troll asked.
"To hone in and improve my ability to walk. I am working on my skills and talent," said the by then 14 years old.

Oleg was by that time already able to walk on his leg braces all the way up to the middle of the mountain. As a matter of fact, the crutches he had dropped altogether from his daily life a while ago.

"Oleg, what is the key ingredient that keeps you making this effort over and over again?" the mountain troll asked.
"Focus. My concentration on my final objective will not change or deviate until I reach the top of the mountain," Oleg said.

By the time he was 16 years old, Oleg attempted the ultimate challenge. He took off his leg braces but hardly could stand much less walk. His by now close companion and admirer the mountain troll was disheartened and pessimistic.
'I had become to believe that he was going to make it to the top, but now?' he mulled over at the sight of the helpless youngster.

Oleg was back to square zero at the bottom of the mountain only able to walk a few hundred meters at the time.

"Are you a masochist? Do you like to suffer or be in pain?" said an obfuscated mountain troll.
"Not in the least, to the contrary I am always happy. My mother says that I was born with an innate sunny disposition for life."

"Well, watching you walk, it sure doesn't look like something joyful to me," said sarcastically the mountain troll.

"Talent and acquired skills driven by focus and concentration are not enough, in addition, I must have the desire and predisposition, the willingness to sacrifice, to endure pain and struggles in the process of learning and improving," said the now 18 years old.

Today, Oleg has finally walked on his own all the way to the top of the mountain atop the Norwegian Fjords and his hometown of Tromso. He has done it, although with great effort, seemingly to the untrained eye, like any other hiker.

"Oleg, my dearest of all friends," starts to say the mountain troll. "What's your secret ingredient? Talent, skills, focus, concentration, readiness to sacrifice, and struggle are not enough. What's the final magic component, the catalyst to all you've accomplished?"

'Passion, Troll, I intensely loved doing what I did and that made me pure and simply Happy!"

Finally, after a long journey that took forever, he gave himself the luxury of riding the cable car down on his way home. The beautiful autumn Nordic sun set in the horizon as the mountain troll waved goodbye to his forever friend, Oleg, the determined youngster from the Norwegian town of Tromso.

"The Sculptor and the Stone"

First, he saw the stone

on a dream…

The next day,

his oneiric experience

morphed into a clear and crisp image,

a vividly and sharp artistic visualization.

The genial artisan

demanded the finest of all marbles,

he expected a stone block with no flaws.

The awesome sculptor

wanted the whitest of all colors.

It's purity and perfection to jump at first sight.

It's smoothness and delicacy to be palpable

and immediately responsive

to his experienced craftsman touch.

His exacting orders were carried out many times over

at the famous Carrara quarries in northern Italy.

But none of the blocks

the masterful artist ever received

met his expectations

hence, they were used for lesser projects.

Then he saw her,

the subject of his work

walking down the street

that ran right in front of his iconic workshop

and straight into Florence's city center.

Her skin seemed like delicate porcelain,

her face features

projected innocence, candor goodness and joy;

Her hair cascaded all the way to her waistline;

Her shape and curves were gentle, soft and classic.

Anatomically and artistically speaking,

she was all he ever wanted.

As time passed by,

the talented artist found himself in a quandary.

He had the idea, and he had the subject

but he did not have the stone.

This, until one good day,

running late to mass,

he found the front door of the cathedral already closed;

running to the sides he looked for an opening;

having found one he rushed in,

but as he was climbing the doorsteps,

he caught a glimpse of it

and stopped right on his tracks.

With eyes of prey,

transfixed,

he moved in deliberate slow motion;

from afar it was hardly visible,

but up close,

right behind the thin layer of underbrush,

there it was,

a large marble stone block

with the whitest of all colors.

Underneath the dirt, time passage and weather traces;

while caressing the stone,

the daring artist was immediately able to feel and touch

the purity and flawlessness of the white marble.

It turned out that the marble stone

had been laying on the side of the cathedral

for decades.

Abandoned right after its arrival,

the commissioned sculptor

had deemed it too narrow

for any work to be done out of it.

Over time the city and its people had simply

forgotten about it.

Weeks later

with city approval

the unwanted rock

was moved to the genial artist's workshop.

Its narrowness to others,

was utter perfection to him.

The masterful sculptor simply saw in the abandoned stone what others didn't.

An even more difficult proposition though,

was to find and persuade his intended muse.

So much so,

that before she ever posed for him

he had to win her heart over;

Along the way she conquered his as well.

So, the bachelor sculptor

and the subject of his artistic desire

ended up marrying each other,

becoming husband and wife.

Sculpting the stone took years;

the passionate artist's chisel

carved, chipped and sandpapered incessantly;

over and over again, every inch of the stone.

It all required precision and accuracy,

any error or mistake

was probably irredeemable and likely irrecoverable.

The stone slowly

morphed progressively

into congruent shapes and forms

ever more challenging;

Yet the artist did it all with joy;

The flow seemed trivially easy;

From the beginning his visualization and preparation

of the work to be done

enabled his subsequent flawless execution;

Also, knowing exactly the stone he needed

and not accepting anything less or different,

allowed him to sculpt it

with comfort, gusto and confidence.

What he didn't expect

or had never experienced before,

was true love.

Besides,

with his model being the subject of his adoration;

a much higher level of passion

permeated and soaked his talents and execution.

Over five centuries old,

the real-life size sculpture

has become a timeless masterpiece;

the beauty of the muse's face

glows under the sparkle of love.

The delicate skin exudes beauty and perfection;

Her figure under rich clothes

can be easily sensed;

Her anatomy stands out for its great detail;

The visible phalanges are all notoriously present;

their silhouettes, posture and positioning

all seem ergonomically alive.

Immortalized forever,

the great sculptor's muse

is a statue symbolizing Love

on all its dimensions into eternity.

The sculptor's greatest achievement though,

consisted in not only bringing his genius along;

including preparing, visualizing and having the right stone;

but while graced with true love as well,

being able to incorporate it in his work;

creating an even higher level of artistic passion,

where the artist achieved

the most sublime connection

between Harmony, Perfection and Love.

And though they stayed together until their passing;

had many children

and he created many other masterpieces;

She only posed for him that once

and he never asked her either;

As true love is neither imitable of replaceable

the sculptor's muse

could only be created once,

forever more.

"Lafitte versus Lafayette"

Deep in the bayou in the Louisiana swamps, the ragged band of outlaws, Buccaneers in the land and the seas, download the riches, they took just a few days ago from a Spanish armada they decimated to nothing in a bloody battle of the seas.

Their leader, dashing Monsieur Lafitte is a sort of Robin Hood taking from some hoarding more than they need, and giving to many others that truly have a use for it.

Tonight, their cache of stolen weapons is changing hands for nothing; along the muddy and still waters, wooden box after wooden box, moves through a human chain, ammunition, muskets, and pistols they contain.

The insurgent smile for the timely receipt of basic supplies from such an unlikely source as Lafitte is the buccaneer, the swash-buckling outlaw, that takes from empires in decline and gives to those building a new one, those freedom fighters fighting to form a mighty country, The United States of America.

Along the shores of the Delaware River, the powerful French Navy flotilla lies in wait in the middle of the night.

The idea and planning for the daring mission has been instigated by a brave visionary and dashing young French military man; a profound "connoisseur" of the affairs of the English colonies and a close collaborator of General George Washington, including his independence movement to free up the colonies from the British crown.

117

Once the French navy meets the rebels, wooden box after wooden box, moves through a human chain ammunition, muskets, and pistols they contain.

The insurgents smile for the timely receipt of basic supplies from such an unlikely source, a swash-buckling French man, The Marquis De Lafayette, an officer from another country's army, who has convinced his own government to give General Washington's freedom fighters' troops, the much-needed armament as they fight to form a mighty country, The United States of America.

"A Noble Mother There Is Only One"

A Noble Mother there is only one,
A Gentle Mother is a treasure we protect and defend to no end,
A doting Mother is always deserving of all our honors, love,
and respect, each day of our lives,
A giving Mother always does EVERYTHING AND
ANYTHING for us,
something we shall never forget to value and recognize.

Her Maternal Instincts never fail,
Her Maternal Judgements either;
She fiercely defends the good and the bad in us regardless
of circumstances,
She always reads us better than anyone,
Correcting and steering us back on track in a snap.
While under her mantle,
No one can feel for us the way she does,
No one can protect us how she does,
Because no one but her
carried and nurtured in her womb that little thing we once were,
Before being born.

An Insanely Awesome Mother she always is,
A Blessing,
A Godly Gift She is,
A Noble, Gentle, Doting, Giving, Insanely Awesome Mother,
She Is Everything There Is.

"The Street Vendor from Portoviejo"

The youngster walks the streets of Portoviejo;
He peddles incessantly,
without a permit,
from sunrise to sundown.

Every day,
early in the morning,
he takes the bus to the city center,
that's where he remains for the rest of the day.

Chestnut unruly hair mops his forehead,
his eyes always looking startled and in awe,
the youngster wears wrinkled short pants,
checkered canvas sneakers,
and the white and diagonal red stripe t-shirt
of the Peruvian National Soccer Team.

The spirited youngster whistles and hums all day long,
always carried by a cheerful spirit,
a steely resolve,
and a sunny disposition
drenched with enthusiasm
towards life and its people.

As long as he can carry the load
throughout the day,
the street vendor normally offers
the kind of products his customers want.

He has an innate pulse for the market;
that's why he's seldom wrong
when he chooses what to sell each day.

What he offers today
seem like ragged strands of cloth and leather
hanging from both sides of his forearms.

Upon closer examination,
what he showcases,
are belts and ties.

But his trade is not free of hiccups.

His main concern
is to stay one step ahead of the police
otherwise, his goods would be immediately confiscated.

He knows the authorities normally look the other way
at what he does.
Yet, one never knows what kind of law enforcement agent
will show up on any particular day…?

His constant fear is not to be robbed
either by his potential clients,
or street criminals
which unfortunately abound
on the city streets.

"There are no better ties and Belts in the market;
I've got them in all sizes and colors,

pick one, two or three
and this could be the day that good fortune smiles at you!"
He peddles incessantly.

Walking by a street café,
unsolicited,
the street vendor approaches a table
where a heavy set man, and an attractive woman
dine outdoors.

Approaching the side of the table
where the inattentive man sits,
the animated youngster displays his belts and ties
by lifting one arm, and then the other.

Initially the heavy set man ignores the youngster,
but when the effusive street vendor insists,
the man angrily waves him off;
and when the persistent youngster tries again,
the heavyset man explodes.

He stands up yelling, cursing and screaming
at the shocked, and scared street peddler.

"Don't you know how to respect people's privacy?"
"Give me one of those," the heavyset man says,
unexpectedly yanking one of the belts
from the youngster's arm.
"This is just trash," he says,
and without even inspecting it,
violently throws the belt to the floor.

"Now, get the hell out of here,"
the angry man yells,
ignoring his female companion lecturing complains.

Dejected the young street vendor
hastily picks up the belt,
and walks hurriedly across the street
where he sits on a bus stop bench.
He looks dejected,
his back hunched and his head down.

At the table the heavy set man
dines with gusto,
until… suddenly, he doesn't.

Right after swallowing
a handful of peanuts
at first, he coughs,
then he begins to choke.

While his companion seems totally helpless,
in a hasty almost violent move,
the heavy set man jumps into a standing position;
frantically flapping his arms
the angry man is unable to breathe.

Across the street the youngster salesman
notices the commotion,
and without thinking runs towards
the choking heavy-set man.

From behind the afflicted man's back
the young street salesman
slides both his arms underneath the armpits
and around the choking man's chest.

But when he tries to lift him up
while applying pressure
to the afflicted man's chest,
the youngster simply cannot do it.
The desperate man is simply too large and heavy.

Undeterred, the youngster releases its grip,
quickly picks-up one of his belts
and again, from behind the choking man's back,
this time he slides the belt around the man's chest.

By pulling both ends of the belt from the back,
The youngster tightens the belt's grip applying pressure
to the man's chest.

The jerky –yet continuous–
tightening and release movements
–also known as the Heimlich maneuver–
seeks to create on the choking man
an urge to throw up.

And so it happens,
The heavy set man coughs out a piece of something
that was choking him;
to the angry man immediate relief,
when it flies out of his mouth unannounced,

magic happens,
the life-death moment vanishes in an instant.

When his focus and attention return,
the heavy set man realizes
that the young street vendor
has in all probably just saved his life.

His expression changes from relief
to embarrassment, then tears of shame;
he walks slowly towards his unlikely savior
with an expression of deep gratitude.

He embraces the youngster tightly
and begins to sob profusely,
finally releasing all the bottled stress and fear
he accumulated while in distress.

"Thank You So Much Miracle Worker,
I did and do not deserve
your good deed, generosity or mercy."

The heavy-set man then sees
all the youngster's belts and ties
spread out and lying on the floor;
without hesitation,
he picks up one by one,
and once organized hands them
to the young street vendor.

While doing so the heavy-set man

vows his head in a sign
of absolute respect
to his generous savior.

"You had the integrity and strength of character
to put aside on an instant
resentment and grudges,
replacing them
with courage and genuine kindness,
both key ingredients of a giving heart,"
It is a life lesson you've have blessed me,
One I will treasure forever more.

"Kindness"

It's the genuine, spontaneous,
humbly, giving gesture.
It's gentle and noble generosity,
It's pious empathy,
It's classy humbleness,
and candor of the heart.
It's uninterested charm,
A rare virtue that does not seeks,
expects or needs a reward.

It's pure love drenched in respect;
It's egoless acts without accolades,
the well-intended deed,
the free-willing, profoundly-wise choice,
where our best attributes and our life's clock,
-driven by the purest forms of love,
and steered by sheer empathy-
are put to good use
for the well-being or betterment of others.

Kindness is a heavenly gift
that is hard to find or give space to
in "the big scheme of things,"

yet it abounds in spades,

and takes place

in the little moments,

in the tiny, bitty details in life,

that's where it resides,

that's where it can be found.

Authentic Kindness,

one of the truest, most precious treasures

we can dote on or put to good use in life.

"Flowers From the Heart"

Small flower arrangements, predominantly roses, show up every morning at each one of the doorsteps of the small suburban community.

Except for the child and his grandma eavesdropping at sunrise, from the Red Victorian house attic, no one else knows who brings the flowers no one is asked to pay for them either.

Yet, they never fail to be, neither to paint bright smiles of joy, as well as happy hearts and chuckles from the fortunate flower recipients.

As he does each and every morning, the humble, wandering man places flower arrangements right at the doorsteps; beautiful red roses prepared and cut with love and tender care.

The man delivering flowers from the heart, lives without a roof over his head; He is disheveled, wears ragged clothes, and noisy, cracked shoes; his bushy hair and beard are tangled and dusty, his strides are bouncy and wayward, yet somehow, they always take him to his intended destination.

"How does he do it?" Asks Jenny, her youngest granddaughter.
"Nobody knows, he is homeless man," replies in amazement Grannie, "One thing I know is that he cannot afford it," Grannie adds.

His big secret is actually not such thing; the secrets of the heart are not hard to fathom if one just looks close enough, but only through the lenses of our own genuine love and affection.

The homeless man rummages and scrabs as he always does, but for the case of his daily offerings, he does it through all of the neighboring town's flower shops dumpsters. There he finds an abundance of discarded flowers, enough to fulfill his purpose and daily good deeds.

"Granny can you see the kind of shoes he wears?"
Jenny asks with shock on her voice.
"Not quite, dear, only that they are quite noisy as he drags them through the floor, what kind of shoes is the homeless man wearing?" Granny asks puzzled.
"Granny, Granny, he's wearing baseball shoes, the homeless man is walking on cleats the whole day long," says and exalted and teary eyed Jenny.
"What a terrible thing for such a good man," observes Granny realizing how cumbersome it must be for the homeless man.
"What should we do Granny, we have to do something!" Jenny says.
"I don't know dear, why should we change anything?
Sometimes giving involves great sacrifices; on the other hand, most of the times we don't appreciate or value what is behind and what does it take for us to receive some of the most wonderful gifts we enjoy," reflects Granny in an open ended fashion.

Impromptu, all of the sudden, the young child pulls her grandmother into a small store.

All excited Jenny asks, chooses and buys the most comfortable shoes the store offers.

Then she runs after the homeless man and offers him the shoes. He seems flustered and indecisive while the young child places the shoes on his hands and runs away immediately back to Granny.

The good man hesitates for a while until he sits down on a bench and tries the shoes and walks a few steps.

His head then turns around slowly
Until he meets the young child eyes.
The homeless man then flashes the brightest and widest of all smiles, and the Young girl smiles back at him trembling with joy and tears.

The homeless man then walks away.
He still has his daily mission to accomplish, but the homeless man knows and is happy about it, that he is now much better prepared to accomplish it.

"The Magic in The Light of A New Day"

Light of Day,

Light of Life,

Light of Dusk,

Light of Dawn,

Light that shines,

Light that brightens

Light that each days follows

"The Circle of Life"

Light that paints life

in a canvas of "Magic Lights"

with a palette of infinite colors,

with endless tones and paint strokes,

Light of Day,

Light of Life,

Light of Dusk,

Light of Dawn.

"Discipline"

Discipline is a virtue we aren't born with.

Hence, it's a code of conduct we have to cultivate,

and work extremely hard for

as we build/growth it into an unassailable HABIT.

When (or until) discipline becomes a deeply ingrained HABIT,

it'll feel heavy,

and a drag that we easily and perennially find excuses to avoid.

To the contrary when it becomes a "kind of" military routine

then it becomes an almost unnoticeable virtue

in the pursuit of endless achievements,

and above all "Excellence"

on anything we embark on in life.

"Impetus"

When desire shines and sparkles,

and yet,

is impregnated with ingenuity and enthusiasm.

When intense energy bursts in spades,

When ebullient predisposition erupts unstoppable,

When our drive is impregnated with "tunnel-vision,"

When we are obsessively "bulls-eye centric,"

while we take action and embark on anything in life,

Impetus is an existentially vital-virtue,

a force to be reckoned with,

as it provides us with indestructible foundations,

supporting an endless inner-strength,

an unwavering, relentless desire,

and an unbreakable, steely determination,

to toil and toil and toil,

until we prevail and conquer,

by reaching our wildest,

our most impossible, improbable dreams;

those extraordinary dreams

where impetus is an essential ingredient,

a required component,

to reach those life-crests,

seemingly unattainable pinnacles,

that only the "impetuous" ride

in the topsy-turvy, merry-go-round

of our precious, but very brief existence.

"Tenacity"

It's Daring with Grit,

It's "Blunt-Boldness" personified,

It's the "Sharpened-Edginess" of Will,

It's ferociousness and fierceness combined.

It's sinking your teeth

into anything in life

with the tightest of all strongholds.

It's the Resilient, Unstoppable Drive,

The Relentless Pursuit,

It's the Tell-Tale of Utter and Sheer Determination,

The Ultimate "Fear-Buster,"

An Irrefutable Demonstration of Valor, and Courage,

The Secret-Ingredient to Break-Out of the mold of Conformism,

while Embracing the Unknown,

It's the "Uncontrollable-Impulse"

to seek out, and explore new things,

while calculating the risks.

It's about how good,

the Quality, and Strength

of our Resilience is,

when facing obstacles and challenges,

it's also about how quickly,

we adapt and react to them,

It's always being prepared to Fail,

while ready to Bounce Right-Back,

and continue trying.

Tenacity is the best formula

to Annihilate and Wipe-Out Uncertainty.

It's one of the most effective methods

to Dissolve and Erase Anxiety,

leaving no room for it to breathe.

Tenaciousness is a Vital Life-Virtue;

the more we put it into practice,

the more Self-Confidence we acquire,

The more Virtuous Circles,

the more Triumphant-Upward-Spirals

we build,

The better Long-Terms Goals we achieve,

The more Opportunities we seize,

The better Chances to create Innovation and Breakthroughs

we earn,

Thus, the bigger our Legacy becomes.

Tenacity is the stuff of Wizards,

a Magic Halo,

the one worn by Life Wizards…

"The Wizards of Life."

"What is Greatness"

Greatness is the ultimate definition of true success!

Greatness is about the impossible,

Greatness is about the improbable,

Greatness is about

finding,

tapping,

uncorking,

deploying,

and fully developing,

the awesome, utter, magical power

of our Geniality.

Greatness is achieved through

the bravest,

fiercest,

most relentless,

ferocious

"Tenacity"

Greatness is

When you soar above the ordinary,

When you excel against all others,

When you surpass all expectations,

When you go beyond your wildest dreams,

When you achieve

seemingly unsurmountable Goals,

Greatness often takes place as well,

when your creations or accomplishments

universally resonate and propagate

while withstanding the passage of time.

On such cases then,

your greatness is revered

while becoming ingrained

in society's folklore and culture.

Greatness provides

the most fulfilling sense of accomplishment,

the intensest

of all spine tingling's.

The sweetest of all shivering's,

swarming all over your body;

an unstoppable rush of feelings and sensations,

a joyous explosion of our deepest passions,

and the bursting realization,

the deepest satisfaction,

of what is

to triumph,

succeed,

vanquish,

and be victorious,

Greatness and Money are like oil and water;

Material riches never engender Greatness.

Knowledge and experience are key ingredients,

but never the catalysts or clinchers

for greatness,

Greatness does not need

an audience,

recognition,

or accolades,

authentic greatness takes place within first,

Hence recognition of greatness by others

although carries respect,

it also bears the ballasts of praise and fame,

which are both fickle, and banal.

Therefore, Genuine greatness

is only a manifestation

of our own inner greatness.

One we are not even aware of,

at first.

Thus, greatness is

first and foremost

an spiritual manifestation,

an introspective discovery,

an attitude that we wear

with pride and honor.

Greatness only happens

when you reach, complete or finish

your odyssey, your journey, your quest.

Right at that moment.

It's the culmination of a long and arduous climb

one where we elevate our levels of excellence

against increasing grades of difficulty

as we navigate through a seemingly

non winnable, endless obstacle course.

Greatness is such memorable instances

when you reach the top of a "hill"

and there's no one there.

At the summit of greatness

you are always alone,

simply because no one else has matched

your feat just yet,

perhaps they'll never do.

There's never an aftermath to Greatness,

as throughout and forever more,

greatness then becomes your credential,

one you'll wear like a badge of honor,

your battle scar,

your rank and file,

your well-deserved proof of ultimate success.

Greatness becomes your persona.

Only those who relentlessly,

dare, chase, persevere, outlast,

and then go where no others are able to,

earn and become bestowed with greatness.

But there is no greatness

without countless, endless, crushing

defeats and failures.

Enduring colossal errors, mistakes, setbacks,

while each and every time,

getting back-up,

followed by "going at it,"

again, and again...

again, and again...,

never, ever giving up.

Foundering is a prerequisite,

an essential building block

for greatness.

When competing,

Greatness happens

when with nothing left in the tank

you still reach out for that extra inch

to cross the finish line ahead of the pack.

Greatness can be

a circumstance,

a moment,

a pinnacle

or a defeat,

it can be a creation in the worlds

of art, words, science,

or simply anything competitive in life,

yet always an accomplishment

resulting out of an extraordinarily resilient effort.

Greatness is never a happenstance

but only the result of

unyielding,

disciplined,

unrepentant,

and obsessively-focused-centered will.

Greatness never happens overnight either,

it takes a really long time, to gain it.

Greatness is what moves and advances humanity forward

by opening new standards and frontiers,

by enriching

our milestones,

treasures,

and legacies.

Greatness is also

One of the telltales of wizards,

"The Wizards of Life."

"The Magical City Busker"

Through winding streets, where echoes play,
A childlike spirit lights the way.
Always smiling, boundless heart,
Sharing art in every part.

He calls himself a busker true,
A private performer just for you.
His songs create collective cheer,
A little boy who holds us near.

From a "Sky Full of Stars" above,
He tries to "Fix Us" with his love.
Sometimes a "Scientist" in thought,
With melodies that heal and teach what can't be taught.

He reminds us "Clocks" are ticking still,
And urges us to "Pray" with will.
He pleads with us to "Vivir la Vida",
To fuel our passions with Reds and "Yellows" of fire,
To love, to dance, to dream, to feel.

He warns that "Every Teardrop Is a Waterfall",
Yet shows us there's "Paradise" for all.
Inviting us to "His Universe",
A place where hope and wonder burst.

Sometimes he just desires to "Talk",
To share a moment on life's walk.
He pleads for us not to "Shiver",

And whispers softly, "Don't Panic", be a giver.

Avoiding paths that lead to "Trouble's" door,
He guides us toward adventures more.
He beckons us to take the ride,
To live life fully, "At the Speed of Light".

He sings of dreams both bold and bright,
A call to hearts lost in the night.
He invites us all to chase the climb,
To join him on "The Adventure of a Lifetime."

Grateful always, inspired still,
He spreads his music, heart and will.
A troubadour without a stage,
His life, a song, a living page.

"Arrogance"

Arrogance is pride, twisted cruel,
A reckless fire, fierce but fueled
By hollow echoes, self-deceit,
A gilded mask with hollow feet.

It struts upon the fragile thread,
A tower built on words unsaid,
Blind to warnings, deaf to grace,
A mirror's love, a lone embrace.

Pride whispers lies— You stand alone!
Yet isolation chills the bone.
It crowns itself in hollow might,
But dims the stars, obscures the light.

With careless scorn, it casts aside
The steady hands that once allied,
Till wisdom flees, till echoes fade,
Till all that's left is loss, betrayed.

Yet where pride crumbles, humbled eyes
Unveil the truth, embrace the wise—
For strength is not the lone command,
But hearts united, hand in hand.

No storm can break the bonds we weave,
No night can steal what we believe.
True power dwells where souls unite,
Where love stands firm, where hearts burn bright.

"The Fall of Lord Avenhurst"

Lord Avenhurst stood atop his grand balcony, gazing over his vast kingdom with satisfaction. His castle, towering over the valley, was a monument to his success—his conquests, his wealth, his unchallenged rule. To him, power was everything, and humility was for the weak.

One day, an old scholar named Elias requested an audience. The man, frail and weathered, was known for his wisdom. Amused, Lord Avenhurst granted him entrance.

"My Lord," Elias said, bowing deeply, "I bring you a warning. The foundation of a kingdom is not stone nor gold, but the loyalty of its people. Treat them with kindness, lest your walls crumble from within."

Lord Avenhurst scoffed. "Loyalty is bought with power, not kindness. My people serve because they fear me. That is enough."

Elias sighed. "A tree stands tall, believing itself indestructible, but it is the unseen rot within that fells it."

The lord dismissed him with a wave.

Seasons passed, and Lord Avenhurst's pride swelled further. He taxed his people heavily, built monuments to himself, and crushed dissent with an iron fist. The more he took, the more he demanded, certain that his power was eternal.

But one winter night, when the castle's golden halls should have glowed with warmth, torches flickered in the distant hills. The people, weary of his rule, had gathered in rebellion. His soldiers, once loyal, abandoned their posts. The walls of his castle, once impenetrable, were thrown open from within.

Lord Avenhurst fled to the highest tower, watching in disbelief as his mighty fortress fell—not to an enemy army, but to the people he had scorned.

As flames licked the sky, he remembered Elias's words. A kingdom is not stone nor gold, but the hearts of those who serve it. And hearts, once turned, will not return.

By dawn, his rule was dust, his pride his downfall.

"The Price of Betrayal"

In the heart of the kingdom of Eldoria,
two warriors stood side by side—
Edric and Rowan—
brothers not by blood, but by bond.
From childhood, they had fought together,
defended their king, and sworn an oath:
"Through steel and storm, together we stand."

But as years passed,
greed whispered to Rowan.
He envied Edric's honor,
the trust the king placed in him.
A shadowed figure came one night,
cloaked in darkness,
offering Rowan a deal—
betray Edric,
and the throne's riches would be his.

Temptation won.

On the eve of battle,
Rowan led Edric into an ambush.
The enemies, waiting in silence, struck.
Edric fought, wounded, his strength fading—
yet his eyes never held anger,
only confusion.
"Why?"
he gasped,
before the final blow fell.

With Edric gone,
the kingdom fell soon after.
The army, once unbreakable,
fractured without its most loyal defender.
The enemy stormed the castle,
the king was slain,
and Rowan, believing himself victorious,
claimed his gold.

Yet power built on treachery is fleeting.
The same shadowed figure
who had bribed him came again—
this time with a better offer for another traitor.
Before the night ended,
Rowan lay in the very spot
where he had betrayed his brother.

The kingdom was lost,
not to a mighty army,
but to a single act of disloyalty.

"The Crown of Loyalty"

Loyalty stands, steadfast and true,
A beacon bright in darkest hue.
Through raging storms, through fire's test,
It guards the heart; it knows no rest.

It is the shield, the sword, the vow,
The hand that lifts, the knee that bows.
It does not waver, break, or bend,
It stands with love, defends a friend.

It binds the hearts that time assails,
A whispered oath that never pales.
Empires rise and empires fall,
But loyalty outlives them all.

It is the root of trust so deep,
The promise made, the bond we keep.
It fuels the light in friendship's eye,
A force that gold can never buy.

It is the fire in honor's name,
The guardian of love's great flame.
Through trials fierce and tempests strong,
Loyalty sings an endless song.

It weaves the threads of home and kin,
Where faith endures and peace begins.
It shields the weak, it lifts the lost,
It asks no price; it counts no cost.

It holds the walls when all seems lost,
It warms the soul through winter's frost.
When shadows fall and hope is thin,
Loyalty fights, it does not dim.

No silver tongue, no treacherous snare,
No whispers false, no lies laid bare,
Can shake its might, can make it yield—
For <u>fidelity</u> never leaves the field.

And in the end, when time is done,
When all is dust, when fades the sun,
The names once carved in fleeting stone
Will fall—but <u>loyalty</u> lives on.

"The Scholar Who Refused the Crown"

They say he lived in the quiet bend of the river,
beneath the flowering plum trees
that leaned gently over his roof like old friends.
His name was not known in cities.
No statues bore his likeness,
no ink sang his praise in ledgers of kings.

But scrolls he wrote were copied in secret
by those who knew where truth slept.
His students came in sandals and silence,
and left with eyes more open than before.

The Court heard whispers.
"A sage," they said, "with clarity rare as spring water in
drought."
And so they sent messengers—
with cloaks of silk and promises dressed in gold.

The first arrived with a jeweled ring.
"The Chancellor's seat is yours," he said,
"if you will only lend your wisdom to the Crown."
The scholar bowed low, and replied,
"A mind in chains cannot think freely.
Let me serve truth, not thrones."

The second came in the rainy season,
offering scrolls inked with titles and honors.
"The world should know your name," she smiled.
"You could guide generations."
He looked at her gently.

"A tree does not ask the wind to carve its name into the
mountain.
Its fruit is proof enough."

The third came cloaked in shadow,
whispers behind him like rustling leaves.
He made no promises.
He spoke instead of what could be lost:
your home, your scrolls, your students…
"Every great oak must bow in a storm."
The scholar lit a lantern,
held it up between them,
and answered softly:
"Then I will be the seed that grows again after fire."

Years passed. The empire changed its shape.
Chancellors fell. Gold grew tarnished.
And the scholar's house remained a little more weathered,
but warm in the glow of morning light.

One day, a young girl knocked at his door.
She carried no titles.
Only questions.
He welcomed her in with a smile
that had never once sought to conquer a crown.

"The Mountain, the Mirror, and the Seed"

In an ancient land where the sky brushed the peaks of towering mountains, there lived a young scholar named Lior. He had mastered the scrolls of every kingdom, debated philosophers into silence, and received honors from kings. And yet, a quiet unease bloomed in his chest—something he couldn't explain.

One day, hearing of a legendary teacher who lived atop the highest peak, Lior set out to climb it. The villagers warned him, "Many go seeking answers, few return the same." But Lior, confident in his intellect, smiled. "I seek truth, not comfort."

After many days, he reached a weathered temple carved into the mountain. Inside, an old woman sat beside a fire. Her robe was simple, her gaze eternal.

"I've come," Lior said, "to learn what remains when all knowledge is known."

The old woman nodded and handed him a mirror, a seed, and a feathered scale.

"Return to me when you understand the weight of these three," she whispered.

Perplexed, Lior descended with the items.

First, he studied the mirror. At first, he saw himself—the confident scholar. But over days, the reflection began to shift. He saw the faces of those he dismissed, ideas he ridiculed, the pride behind his wisdom. The mirror showed not his image, but his impact.

Then came the seed. He planted it in rich soil, watering and watching. But it did not grow. Frustrated, he examined it closely—only to realize it was hollow. He wept, understanding only honesty bears fruit. Like the seed, knowledge without humility is empty.

Last, the feathered scale. He placed his accolades on one side—scrolls, trophies, praise—and stood on the other. The scale did not tip. But when he placed the mirror and the seed on his side, it slowly bowed toward him. He realized: humility isn't measured by what we carry, but by what we're willing to leave behind.

Years passed. When Lior returned to the mountain, he was no longer adorned in silk or certainties. The old woman smiled, offering him tea.

"What have you learned?" she asked.

"That wisdom is not in knowing more," he said, "but in needing less. That humility is not silence, but the refusal to place oneself above truth. That a seed, though silent, can split stone—and a mirror, though still, can crack arrogance."

The old woman nodded. "Then you may stay. Or return. Your choice is no longer driven by the need to be right—but by the grace to be whole."

Moral of the Fable: Humility is not the denial of worth, but the deep knowing that truth is never owned—only served. It is in the empty seed, the honest mirror, and the balanced scale that we learn: the greatest weight we bear is not what we know, but what we've yet to unlearn.

"The Lake and the Stream"

In the heart of a lush valley, there lay a beautiful, tranquil lake, fed gently by a lively, spirited stream. The lake was vast, reflecting the clouds and stars, admired by every creature nearby. The stream, though smaller and narrower, sparkled with ceaseless movement, dancing between rocks, its waters always clear and alive.

One day, the lake spoke to the stream with certainty, "Why do you rush so restlessly, dear stream? Look at me—I am calm, stable, admired by all who gaze upon my beauty. Your endless agitation seems foolish."

The stream chuckled gently, replying, "I must flow, for movement is my nature. Without it, I would lose all I cherish."

The lake laughed softly, dismissing the stream's words as restless folly. Years passed, and the stream continued to flow joyously, nurturing flowers, wildlife, and trees along its banks. It remained ever fresh and vibrant, admired for its pure, crystal-clear waters.

But the lake, content in its stillness, gradually changed. Its calm waters slowly darkened, becoming clouded by weeds and algae. Fish avoided it, birds no longer nested along its shores, and the animals ceased visiting. The stagnant waters, once so admired, turned stale and murky.

Eventually, saddened and puzzled by its solitude, the lake called out to the stream again, "Friend, tell me, why has the world turned away?"

The stream, still lively and fresh, replied softly, "Dear lake, beauty without movement fades into decay. You chose calm without growth, tranquility without renewal. Life thrives in motion."

Realizing the truth too late, the lake asked mournfully, "Is there hope left for me?"

The stream comforted the lake gently, saying, "It is never too late to renew. If you let me flow through you once more, perhaps together we can restore your vitality."

Humbled, the lake opened itself to the stream's refreshing waters, and slowly, life returned. Fish swam, birds sang, and animals gathered once more. Though the lake never forgot the lesson of stagnation, it lived thereafter in grateful harmony with the stream—ever moving, ever growing.

Moral of the Fable: Stagnation, however comfortable, leads inevitably to decay; only through continual movement and renewal does life flourish.

"Dreamers Forge the World"

We are the whispers in the dark,
The gentle sparks that light the flame,
We dare the unseen roads embark,
Inventing
pathways without name.

With minds unbound, horizons wide,
In shadows deep we plant the seed,
Through possibility we stride,
For every need birth greater deed.

A thousand roads before us part,
Yet courage guides our restless feet,
For innovation stirs the heart—
The music makers' pulse and beat.

We challenge comfort's sleepy reign,
In every limit, break the mold,
Transforming loss to hopeful gain,
Turning leaden dreams to gold.

We dwell where chance and vision blend,
Crafting future from desire,
Within imagination's bend,
We shape the world with endless fire.

Innovation, simply said,
Is daring thought made manifest,
Transforming visions in our head,

To living truths, life's brightest quest.

We risk, defiant to the scorn,
Unshaken by the skeptic's call,
In faith of what is yet unborn,
Believing dreams despite them all.

Remember this, embrace the light,
Each dream pursued renews the earth,
For progress blooms from courage bright—
Innovation shapes rebirth.

So dream, create, and boldly strive,
Let courage write your lasting rhyme,
Through innovation we survive—
In changing, we defy all time, forevermore.

Moral of the Poem: Stagnation, however comfortable, leads inevitably to decay; only through continual movement and renewal does life flourish.

"The Owl and the Shrouded Forest"

In an ancient forest veiled in endless twilight, shadows whispered softly, weaving tales of fear and ignorance. Trees stood solemn and silent, their branches heavy with resignation, their roots bound by apathy. They spoke as one, "The dark has always been our home. To question is perilous; better to accept what is known."

Yet amid this dimness lived Lira, a curious owl with feathers like silver moonlight and eyes bright as stars. Restless and unafraid, she peered into the gloom, her heart burning with a single question: "Why must we dwell forever in darkness?"

The forest groaned dismissively, leaves rustling in disdain, "Curiosity brings danger. Do not disturb what has always been."

But Lira could not silence the yearning that stirred within her. Driven by the need to understand, she spread her wings and soared into the very heart of darkness, deeper than any creature had dared to go. There, hidden behind tangled branches and ancient thorns, she found a secluded glade illuminated by the faint glow of a solitary star.

In the glade lay a shroud woven thickly from threads of ignorance and fear, pulsing like a living entity. As Lira approached, shadows hissed fiercely, "Accept the darkness! Return to safety!"

Yet Lira's curiosity was stronger than fear. Determined, she called out to the creatures of the forest, urging them to share her question. Foxes crept forward bravely, hares stepped forth with wary hope, and ravens descended from their high perches, driven by a

168

newfound hunger for truth. Together, paw by claw by wing, they began to unravel the shroud.

Slowly at first, then faster, the threads of ignorance loosened and fell away. With every thread removed, more light poured into the glade, spreading warmth and illumination throughout the forest. At last, brilliant sunlight broke through, bathing the trees in golden radiance.

Awakened from their long, passive slumber, the trees stirred in awe, leaves shimmering in wonder. They whispered softly to Lira, "We were wrong to fear questions. You have taught us to seek, to learn, to illuminate our world."

Perched on a branch in the heart of the forest, now vibrant with life and light, Lira gazed upon her community renewed. "Curiosity," she declared softly, yet firmly, "is the beacon that dispels darkness. Together, our questions become the light by which truth is revealed."

Moral: Curiosity, when pursued bravely and shared openly, lifts the veil of ignorance, illuminating paths to wisdom and enlightenment.

Moral of the Fable: Curiosity, pursued in unity, peels back ignorance's layers, revealing a brighter reality.

"The Lantern of Inquiry"

In a realm of shadowed halls,

where whispers cloaked the light,

a lantern burned, its flame so small,

yet piercing through the night.

It sought the hidden, the unseen,

through corridors of doubt,

each question a spark, a glowing gleam,

to drive the darkness out.

The shadows hissed, "Accept our shade!"

but the lantern's flame grew bold,

its curious light refused to fade,

unveiling truths untold.

It called to hearts, "Come, seek with me!"

and hands joined one by one,

their questions a song, a shared decree,

till dawn's first light was won.

A daring hunger burned within,

a thirst to know, to see;

they risked the safety of the dim

for truths that set them free.

With restless hearts, they chased the glow,

no boundary could restrain;

an itch to learn, to brave and grow,

ignited each new flame.

Forever burns this daring fire,

an endless blaze of quest,

for curiosity's desire

awakens life's unrest.

Moral of the Poem: Curiosity, like a lantern's flame, illuminates the shadows of ignorance, guiding shared hearts to truth through persistent questioning.

"The Sparrow and the Valley of Stone"

In the Valley of Stone, sunlight burned relentlessly, leaving the earth cracked and lifeless. Here dwelled creatures whose hearts had long ago dried into hard shells of indifference. Lizards basked alone on brittle rocks, coyotes prowled in bitter solitude, and even the cacti stood rigid, their spines sharp and unyielding. "It has always been so," they murmured, resigned to a world drained of tenderness.

Yet into this parched world fluttered Elara, a small sparrow with feathers the color of dawn and a heart radiant with compassion. Wherever she flew, she spread whispers of hope, but they scattered on deaf ears and closed hearts. Undeterred, Elara searched tirelessly, sensing a hidden truth beneath the barren land.

The hot winds mocked her efforts, hissing cruelly through the valley, "Give up, foolish bird. Compassion cannot soften stone."

Still, Elara refused to yield. One starlit night, guided by her unshakable empathy, she felt a pulse beneath the valley's crust, like the distant heartbeat of the earth itself. Landing softly, she pecked gently at the ground. Soon, a trickle emerged, tiny but miraculous—a secret spring concealed deep below.

The creatures watched skeptically. "It will vanish," hissed the lizard. "It is nothing but trickery," growled the coyote. Yet, day by day, Elara continued her humble work, carefully widening the tiny source with tireless effort.

Gradually, curiosity softened the valley's hardened inhabitants. The cactus leaned closer, offering shade to the tireless sparrow. The lizard, intrigued by her perseverance, cleared loose pebbles from her path. The coyote, moved by her gentle strength, dug into the hard earth beside her. Through shared purpose, claws and spines, paws and feathers united in harmony, each creature contributing what it could.

Finally, the spring surged forth, clear and abundant, cascading joyously into the valley. Life blossomed rapidly, softening not only the land but also the once-callous hearts of those who lived there. Flowers bloomed where despair had taken root, laughter echoed where silence had reigned, and the once-solitary beings discovered the warmth of community.

Elara, her mission fulfilled, perched contentedly upon a flowering branch. "Compassion," she sang gently, "is the hidden water that nourishes all life. Together, we flourish. Divided, we wither."

And from that day forward, the Valley of Stone was remembered not for its callous past, but as the Valley of Renewal, where compassion flowed as freely as the waters that restored their world.

Moral of the fable: Compassion, shared with courage and unity, can transform even the hardest hearts and most barren landscapes into flourishing worlds of renewed hope and connection.

"The Shroud of Indifference"

In winter's grip a shroud was spun,

A veil of ice concealing pain,

Where frozen hearts had turned away,

Blind eyes ignoring others' strain.

Silent suffering lingered unseen,

Cries muffled beneath frosty lace,

Cold indifference held the world,

Empathy vanished without a trace.

Yet deep within the brittle chill,

A single spark began to glow—

The quiet warmth of tender care,

A seed of kindness in the snow.

It spread gently from heart to heart,

Melting callous ice with grace,

Until compassion thawed the frost,

Revealing truths, we now embrace.

As warmth dissolved the icy veil,

Illusions shattered, clear and bright:

When hearts unite in empathy,

They bring the world from dark to light.

No cruelty stands where love resides,

No frost remains where kindness grows—

Compassion heals, compassion guides,

And through its strength, humanity flows.

Moral: Even the deepest frost of indifference cannot withstand the gentle warmth of compassion, for when hearts unite in empathy, healing and hope prevail.

"The Tree of Echoes: A Fable of Injustice and Hope"

In a valley nestled between two great mountains stood the Village of Mirrors. The villagers lived harmoniously, reflecting kindness upon one another. At the heart of this village grew the Tree of Echoes, whose silver leaves whispered truths and whose golden fruits nourished fairness.

One day, a shadow entered the valley—a traveler cloaked in darkness named Injustice. He carried a staff carved from deception, and wherever he walked, flowers wilted and whispers fell silent.

Injustice approached the Tree of Echoes, disturbed by its truthfulness. He struck it with his staff, causing cracks to appear along its bark. Leaves fell silently to the ground, turning to ash upon touch. "Your fairness is a burden," he hissed. "I will silence your echoes."

The villagers gathered, alarmed, but fear silenced their voices. Each waited for another to act, and in this hesitation, the shadow grew stronger. The once radiant valley dimmed, its mirrors tarnished, reflecting only confusion and doubt.

Yet, from beneath the fractured roots emerged a small, golden seed. A young girl named Aletheia, who had seen truth silenced and fairness wounded, took the seed gently in her palm. Guided by courage, she planted it at the valley's edge, nurturing it secretly with tears and whispers of hope.

Slowly, a new tree rose—a quiet sentinel growing with resilience. Its bark was humble yet strong, and its fruits modest but sustaining.

176

As villagers tasted the fruit, their voices returned, clearer and stronger than before. Realizing their error, they faced Injustice united.

"You fed on our silence," Aletheia declared. "But truth cannot be broken. Even from the smallest seed, justice rises again."

Defeated by the power of unity and truth, Injustice withdrew, vanishing beyond the mountains.

From then onward, the villagers cherished the humble tree, understanding that justice thrives not by grandeur, but by courage and vigilance in the hearts of those who speak, even when their voices tremble.

Moral of the Fable: Justice cannot be permanently silenced or destroyed; it emerges resiliently from even the smallest acts of courage and truth. The strength of justice lies not in grandeur, but in the quiet, unwavering bravery of those who dare to speak and act despite fear or uncertainty. Ultimately, unity and collective courage hold the power to overcome injustice and restore harmony.

"The Lake of Fair Reflections"

In a land veiled by mist, there lay a hidden lake, waters pure as crystal, reflecting only truth.

At the lake's edge, three creatures gathered— Fox, Raven, and Deer— each seeking justice, for bias had spread like a sickness through their land.

Fox spoke first, his voice smooth as silk: "Justice favors the cunning, for wisdom outsmarts strength." Yet, when he peered into the lake, his reflection trembled, blurred by hidden deceit.

Then Raven cawed, sharp and harsh: "Justice belongs to the loudest, those who claim it first." But upon the water, her image twisted, a shadow of arrogance.

Finally, Deer stepped forward, gentle eyes wide and clear. "Justice is neither cunning nor loud, it listens quietly, and speaks softly, it walks humbly but stands firm."

As Deer gazed down, the waters stilled, her reflection clear, pure and undistorted.

Then the lake spoke, its voice calm and deep: "True justice reflects not the loudest cry, nor the cleverest mind, but fairness— an honest mirror free of bias.

Justice is the impartial and honest recognition of truth, a principle rooted in fairness, equality, and integrity, ensuring each voice is heard and every action weighed without prejudice.

Justice is the impartial and honest recognition of truth, a principle rooted in fairness, equality, and integrity, ensuring each voice is heard and every action weighed without prejudice.

Justice is balance, a careful weighing of rights and wrongs. It knows no favorites, no ranks, no disguises. It seeks truth over comfort, and clarity over noise. Justice is courage, to stand for another's truth as strongly as one's own."

Fox and Raven bowed, learning humility, and beside Deer, they returned home, carrying the lesson.

Moral of the Fable: Justice shines brightest when fairness conquers bias, and truth speaks in whispers that every heart can hear.

"The Raven and the Shattered Cliff"

In a village cast in the long shadow of a jagged cliff, fear ruled as a sovereign. Every creak of stone, every gust of wind sparked dread among the people, who huddled in silence, whispering of collapse. Legends turned the cliff into a monster—not of rock, but of imagined doom. Their trembling hearts fractured the ground more than time or tremor ever could.

High above them, in a pine that leaned bravely into the sky, lived Veyra, **a lone raven with feathers like storm-slick stone and eyes dark with insight**. She watched as fear wrapped itself around the villagers like fog, thickening each day. "Why," she asked the wind, "do they fear what they've not dared to know?"

The villagers rebuked her calm. "To be afraid is to be safe," they chorused. Yet beneath their words, the earth groaned—less from the weight of the cliff than the weight of worry. As they tiptoed away from danger, their retreat loosened the soil beneath them.

Veyra took flight.

She did not flee, but flew closer—to the cliff, to the truth. Through biting winds and echoing warnings, she circled and descended on a jutting ledge, scarred yet firm. Her wings furled, her gaze unwavering, she stood sentry as the night howled.

One by one, villagers looked up.

Not all at once, but in small ripples of courage, hearts stirred by Veyra's defiance of dread. A young shepherd was first to climb, then a stonemason, then a widow with shaking hands. Together, they joined her on the ledge—not because it was safe, but because it was solid, and because their unity made it stronger still.

With each step taken in courage, the cliff ceased its moans. The ground quieted. The wind, once fierce, now carried the song of a people no longer hiding.

They rebuilt—not beneath the shadow, but beside the strength. And at the cliff's foot, where fear once ruled, rose a gathering of souls, brave not because they felt no fear, but because they chose not to bow to it.

And so it was that Veyra, the raven of the unshaken pine, taught a trembling world that fortitude is not loud, but luminous. It does not roar, it perches. And it waits—not to be followed, but to be understood.

Moral of the Fable: Fear, left unchecked, multiplies the very danger it hopes to avoid. But fortitude—especially when shared— turns trembling into trust and panic into strength. Courage does not mean the absence of fear, but the choice to rise above it. When people stand together, even cliffs once feared begin to stand still.

"The Flame of Resolve"

In lands were silence stifled breath,

and stars withdrew in fright,

where dread distilled the scent of death

and day dissolved to night,

there stirred a flame no storm could snuff,

no whisper could dismay—

a sovereign spark, though small enough,

it would not turn away.

It shimmered on a shattered wall,

where once bold voices spoke;

it dared to rise though fears would crawl

and cloak the air in smoke.

The void hissed threats in every gust—

"Extinguish! Or obey!"

But fire, when born of sacred trust,

will never turn to gray.

Through thunder's wrath and shadow's leer,

it danced in calm defiance—

not loud, but deep, not loud, but clear—

a flame of self-reliance.

Its glow did not demand a throne,

nor wait for tides to shift;

it lit the path for those alone,

a bridge, a buoy, a gift.

One watched. Then two. Then throngs drew near,

each soul with burdened eyes,

yet in the flame's unblinking cheer,

they saw their own arise.

The timid hand, once clenched in fright,

now reached to shield the flame;

each breath it drew gave birth to light,

and none remained the same.

The darkness, vast as ocean's hold,

now thinned with every gleam—

for fire that's shared grows not old,

but lives in shared esteem.

And so, the cliff did cease to crack,

the wind no longer moaned;

for hearts alight will not fall back

when fear stands not alone.

Now etched in stone where once was dread,

these words in embers burn:

"Let courage walk where fear once tread—

and hope will not return.

For though the night may rise again

with storms yet unrevealed,

the flame of fortitude in men

will stand. And never yield."

Moral of the Poem: Fear isolates, feeding on silence and doubt. But fortitude, like a flame, awakens others—not through force, but by its example. When even one soul dares to burn against the dark, it gives others permission to rise, and together, they become the dawn.

"The Council of Mirrors"

In an ancient city veiled in perpetual fog, where light struggled to pierce the gloom, a solemn council of elders convened in a marble hall. Each elder held a mirror—ornate, silver-framed, and untouched. They had been given these mirrors not for vanity, but for wisdom. Yet none dared gaze into them.

The city had grown restless. Whispers turned into accusations. Blame passed from mouth to mouth like a torch, burning bridges between neighbors. In their great chamber, the elders quarreled: "You've sown the seeds of discord!" said one. "It is your ambition that darkens our streets!" barked another. And always, their mirrors remained veiled in cloth, hidden in fear.

One evening, a traveler entered the city—cloaked not in silk or armor, but in clarity. He listened in silence, then spoke, not with judgment, but with calm:

"You speak of shadows, yet none of you has faced your own."

He motioned to their covered mirrors.

"You carry the light you deny yourselves."

His words stung, not with cruelty but with truth. Unease swept the chamber. One elder—a once-proud woman whose voice had grown sharp—was the first to unveil her mirror. She gasped. Not at age, but at anger etched into her eyes. Another followed, and another. One by one, they dared to look—and what they saw was not guilt, but grief. Not malice but misunderstanding. Their own reflections revealed truths they had long buried beneath the clamor of certainty.

Tears fell—quietly, without spectacle. And as they wept, something miraculous occurred: the fog outside began to thin. Light filtered into alleys. Windows gleamed again. Laughter returned to courtyards.

The council did not declare a victor. They embraced silence, then forgiveness. For the first time in generations, they saw one another not as foes, but as mirrors—each reflecting the potential for both fracture and healing.

From that day forward, when discord threatened the city, the council did not raise voices. They raised mirrors. And in the stillness of self-recognition, they found peace.

Moral of the Fable: True clarity begins not by judging others, but by confronting our own reflection. When we dare to see ourselves honestly, conflict loses its grip. Reflection is not weakness—it is the quiet virtue that turns fear into wisdom and division into unity.

"The Shared Well"

In a sun-scorched land, a community found its single source of water in a deep stone well. Drought loomed, and each family feared losing what little remained. In desperation, some tried to hoard containers of water, hiding them behind locked doors. Others sabotaged neighbors' buckets, hoping to conserve more for themselves.

One scorching morning, a young child stumbled to the well, parched and weak. Though her family had tried saving water, they had exhausted their ration. Seeing her desperation, an elderly man who had a few extra scoops left offered them willingly. Witnessing this generosity, others stepped up to share, first timidly, then with unguarded hearts.

Despite the drought, the well's supply endured longer than anyone expected. With each shared scoop, gratitude replaced fear, forging bonds where suspicion had festered. When precious rainfall finally returned, the entire village celebrated not just water, but the generosity that had saved them from despair.

From that day forward, the well was never hoarded again. Each villager remembered that when one among them thirsted, all were at risk of withering. And so, they passed along this lesson: in giving, we preserve life; in hoarding, we sow desolation."

Moral of the Fable: In times of scarcity, survival depends not on selfishness but on shared compassion—when we give to others in need, we nourish the whole community and keep hope alive.

"Voices Divided"

A prosperous city became mired in dispute when half the council demanded exclusive rights to new lands, while the other half insisted such grants would exploit the poor. Meetings turned heated, each side casting accusations.

In the midst of this uproar, a wise mediator arrived with a single question: "How can you govern fairly if you refuse to hear each other's plight?" The council laughed at the notion of listening to opponents. But the mediator stood firm, proposing a day for each side to speak uninterrupted while the other listened in silence.

Reluctantly, the council agreed. By day's end, both factions realized they misunderstood each other's fears and hopes. The wealthy feared losing established privileges, while the struggling families feared permanent disenfranchisement. With the mediator's guidance, they drafted a charter ensuring reasonable land access for all—a balance preserving the city's prosperity without trampling the vulnerable.

Once the charter passed, tension ebbed. Residents found renewed trust in their leaders, and the city thrived. The council, though still opinionated, embraced a rule: no law could pass without hearing each voice in turn. Fairness had prevailed over division.

Moral of the Fable: Harmony begins with listening—only by truly hearing one another can opposing sides transform conflict into fair and lasting solutions.

"The Two-Factions"

A great city was divided into two factions: the High Terraces, where nobles lived, and the Low Fields, home to laborers. Tensions escalated, as the nobles passed laws favoring themselves, while the laborers seethed at the injustice.

One day, a traveling judge arrived, summoned by the pleas of the Low Fields. She convened both sides in an open forum, placing a single chair at the center. "Let none speak until you can do so sitting in this chair," she declared. Curiosity gripped the crowd, for the seat seemed too small for either side to claim alone. Noble leaders tried to sit but found the seat tilted precariously whenever they didn't share space. The laborers, too, discovered they couldn't balance it alone. Finally, one noble and one laborer approached together, each sharing half the chair. To their surprise, it remained steady.

The judge proclaimed, "Justice requires no side to tower above the other. Only when we share the space of debate can we stand firm." Realizing this truth, the factions began rewriting laws to address both privileged concerns and daily hardships, forging solutions that benefited all.

Henceforth, the city's council sessions always included a balanced seat to remind everyone: if one side claims it all, both sides fall.

Moral of the Fable: Lasting justice is built not through dominance but through shared understanding—only when opposing sides sit together in balance can a society truly stand strong.

"The Stormbound Guardian"

A coastal city built its timekeeping tower on a high bluff, reliant on a single clock to warn sailors of the tides. One fateful year, a fierce tempest loomed—thunder roiled, lightning split the horizon, and monstrous waves surged. In panic, most fled inland, abandoning the clock.

Yet a solitary guardian remained. Despite the howling winds and lashing rain, she refused to leave her post, knowing that if the clock failed, ships at sea would have no signal of safe harbor. Fear clawed at her mind, urging her to retreat to shelter, but she steadied her trembling hands.

Hour by hour, she reinforced the tower's beams, shielding the clock's mechanism from raging waters. Lightning scorched the sky, debris hammered the walls, yet she persevered. When dawn broke, battered and soaked, she rang the bell—alerting ships to return home. The city realized her courage saved hundreds of lives. Ever after, the townspeople told of the guardian who stood unyielding, reminding all that real bravery isn't the absence of terror, but the triumph of resolve over surrender."

Moral of the Fable: True bravery lies not in being fearless, but in standing firm when fear tempts retreat—one resolute spirit can safeguard many when all others turn away.

"The Tempest Guardian"

In a coastal city famed for its monumental clock tower, a monstrous storm once threatened to wash everything away—livelihoods, homes, and hope. As frightened citizens evacuated, one humble watchman remained. Through driving rains and howling gales, he stood at the tower's base, repairing splintered gears and draining floodwater that seeped inside.

Hour after hour, winds battered him. Thunder rattled the tower's stones, and shards of wind-driven debris bruised his arms. Yet each time he faltered, the watchman remembered that ships at sea relied on this clock for tide signals. If it failed, more lives would be lost. So he pressed on, determined to keep the clock ticking.

At dawn, the storm subsided. The clock's chimes rang out over a battered but unbroken city. Its people returned to find that, despite the furious tempest, their timekeeper still stood. The watchman had endured every hardship, for he refused to let despair claim that vital heartbeat of their community."

Moral of the Fable: Steadfast commitment in the face of adversity can preserve the rhythm of hope—when one person holds firm for the sake of many, even the fiercest storms cannot silence the heartbeat of a community.

"The Windswept Beacon"

In a rugged coastal region, a colossal beacon tower once guided ships through relentless storms. When a cataclysmic gale struck, the keeper faced floodwaters racing in, threatening to drown the machinery that operated the beacon's revolving light. For two days, the keeper fought exhaustion, manning a manual crank whenever the engine sputtered. Rain battered his every breath, salt spray stung his eyes. More than once he nearly collapsed, but he recalled the ships depending on that glow to find safe harbor.

At dusk on the second day, the storm peaked, slamming the beacon with waves tall as houses. Despite trembling hands and a battered body, the keeper refused to abandon his post. He cranked again, sweat and rain mingling on his brow. Finally, at dawn, the storm lifted. The beacon still turned, and countless vessels had avoided disaster.

From then on, local lore held that no gale could break a spirit fused to a greater cause. Where hopelessness demanded surrender, the keeper persisted—his light never fully dimmed."

Moral of the Fable: Unyielding dedication to a purpose greater than oneself can outlast even the fiercest storms—true perseverance becomes a guiding light for others when all seems lost.

"The Celestial Weave"

In an age before clocks and compasses, twelve shining virtues danced among the stars—courage sparked bright as dawn, justice balanced the heavenly scales, generosity gave a nurturing warmth, and perseverance refused to yield. Compassion bound broken souls, curiosity lit unknown roads, fortitude withstood every storm, while humility kept pride at bay.

Yet these virtues spun alone, each a separate orb adrift in cosmic gloom. Twisting shadows rose, dividing hearts and warping realms. With no unity to brace them, the virtues began to splinter under illusions' weight.

One lonely star saw the fracture and reached out. Slowly, each virtue found a common melody. Courage welcomed justice's balance, generosity soothed resentment, and curiosity embraced empathy. They spun again, not as lone lights, but as a single constellation. Shadows broke apart, their dividing whispers silenced.

In that cosmic dawn, the virtues, once fractured, shone as one blazing light—unity's eternal flame, forging a tapestry that no dark illusions could tear apart.

Moral of the Fable: Only through unity can individual strengths become an unbreakable force—when virtues weave together in harmony, they dispel even the deepest shadows and illuminate a path beyond illusion.

"The Dusk of Fracture, the Dawn of One"

Before ages were tallied and clocks first chimed, twelve radiant virtues danced among uncounted stars. Courage lit a bold flame, while justice balanced each cosmic scale. Generosity flowed to mend lonely hearts, as perseverance refused to break beneath storms. Compassion stirred healing, curiosity probed every dawn, and fortitude stood steadfast against fear's gnawing night. Innovation birthed brighter paths, humility steered proud souls, wisdom guided mortal wonder, rationality brought clarity, and unity bridged them all.

Then came a fell time when each virtue spun alone, trapped in illusions of division. Shadows whispered, "Stand apart," until even starlight dimmed. Yet from that gloom arose a single star, remembering how each virtue once shone in unison. One by one, the virtues bent close, forming a constellation no darkness could undo. In that dawn, illusions scattered, for unity bound every ember into an unbreakable blaze. What had fractured was forged anew, the dawn of one unstoppable light.

Moral of the Fable: Even the brightest virtues lose their power in isolation, but when reunited in harmony, they become a force capable of dispelling darkness and healing what once was broken.

"A Cosmos Renewed"

In eras marred by fractures, illusions spun webs that severed hearts, cloaking each virtue in shadow. Courage faltered, justice dimmed, generosity shrank into greed. From shattered fragments, a lone star recalled how once they shone together, forging an unbreakable bond that illusions could not breach.

Across distant lands, each virtue awakened anew—perseverance reignited hope, compassion bridged wounds, curiosity sparked new dawns, and fortitude steadied fearful hearts. With every step, illusions lost their sting as synergy surged. At last, at the cosmic Orloj of unity, these virtues converged, forming a radiant tapestry that illusions found impossible to tear.

In that final convergence, division's last stronghold collapsed, undone by the knowledge that every strength was multiplied in union. The cosmos breathed again, no corner left to illusions' hush. From the arcs of synergy rose an eternal flame—twelve lights fused into one, bright enough to guide worlds beyond illusions' reach.

Moral of the Fable: *True strength is born not in isolation but in unity—when virtues align and work in harmony, they dispel the illusions that divide us and illuminate a path to lasting renewal.*

"The Spark of the Unknown"

In a forest bound by shadow,
where roots clung to ancient soil,
stagnation reigned, its grip unyielding,
leaves unturned, paths unseen.

A spark awoke, a flicker small,
born of a restless wind,
it danced through brambles,
igniting trails where none had been.
The trees, once rigid, bent to see,
their branches stretching toward the light,
new growth unfurled, green and bold,
as the spark carved rivers of change.

The forest breathed, its stillness broken,
a symphony of growth and motion,
where once was silence, now a song—
innovation's fire, burning strong.

Moral: Innovation, like a spark in darkness, ignites progress
where stagnation seeks to bind.

"The River and the Stone"

In a verdant valley where mountains kissed the sky, a river flowed, its waters clear and humble, nourishing all in its path. At the valley's heart stood a stone, ancient and unyielding, its surface etched with veins of gold—corruption's gleam. The stone demanded tribute from the creatures of the valley, promising wealth but damming the river's flow, choking life from the land.

The river, undeterred, spoke softly, "I seek only to flow, to give, not to take." The stone laughed, its voice a grating echo. "Bow to me, or dry to dust." But the river, with quiet resolve, pressed on, its waters lapping at the stone's edges, day after day, year after year. Its humility wore down the stone's corruption, eroding its golden veins until it crumbled, its greed washed away.

The valley bloomed anew, the river's humble flow restoring life, its modesty a testament to enduring strength.

Moral: Humility, like a river's steady flow, overcomes corruption's unyielding barriers.

"Shadows of Superstition"

In the lush valley of Eldermoor nestled between towering mountains, lay the peaceful village of Ravenshade. Life flowed calmly, nourished by clear streams and fertile fields, until one ominous morning a rare celestial event darkened the sky—a blood-red eclipse that cast the village into shadow. Terrified, villagers believed it was an evil omen foretelling doom, spreading panic and despair.

Amidst this hysteria lived Astraea, a young scholar known for her boundless curiosity and sharp intellect but viewed skeptically by villagers wary of her unusual contraptions and endless scrolls. As fear spread, superstitions flourished. Crops withered untended, children huddled indoors, and whispers of evil curses echoed through the streets.

Determined to dispel ignorance, Astraea set forth into the forbidden Great Library of Eldermoor, a ruin said to be haunted by vengeful spirits. Ignoring the warnings, she spent days deciphering ancient texts under flickering lanterns, meticulously unraveling the science behind the crimson eclipse. She discovered that such an event was merely a celestial alignment, predictable and harmless, a phenomenon known by scholars of old.

Returning to Ravenshade, Astraea called a gathering beneath the village's great oak. Facing skepticism, she demonstrated her findings with clear explanations and careful diagrams. Yet doubt lingered—fear was deep-rooted, difficult to uproot.

Undeterred, Astraea proposed a test. Consulting her calculations, she accurately predicted another eclipse, convincing a hesitant populace to witness this natural wonder without fear. When the predicted eclipse unfolded exactly as foretold, wonder replaced dread. Realizing their error, the villagers felt ashamed yet enlightened.

Grateful, Ravenshade embraced knowledge over superstition, pledging never again to let fear eclipse reason. From that day, Astraea's name was celebrated, and the village flourished, becoming renowned as a beacon of enlightenment.

Thus, Ravenshade learned an invaluable lesson:

Knowledge shines brightest where fear's shadow is darkest.

Moral: True understanding dispels ignorance, freeing the heart and mind from the chains of superstition and fear.

"Beacon of Reason"

In gardens of the mindful heart,
Where reason plants its seed,
Rationality blooms and thrives,
Dispelling fear and need.

Like sailors guided by stars,
On tempest-ridden seas,
Rationality charts our course,
With logic as the breeze.

Within the labyrinth of doubt,
It lights the way ahead,
As Ariadne's silken thread,
Ensures we're never misled.

Rationality, clear and sound,
Weighs evidence precise,
Judgment formed by careful thought,
Avoiding false advice.

The mind—a blacksmith at its forge,
Shapes truths from molten thought,
Crafting knowledge firm and pure,
From clarity it's wrought.

In darkness deep as moonless night,
It shines a lantern's beam,
Banishing shadows cast by myths,
Awakening from dreams.

A bridge between belief and truth,
Built stone by careful stone,
Rationality leads us forth,
To wisdom rarely known.

It's compass needle, steady, sure,
Points to the north of fact,
Freeing souls from superstition's grip,
And fear's oppressive pact.

Yet like a gardener diligent,
We must nurture it with care,
For reason left neglected,
Withers in despair.

Rationality's not cold nor cruel,
But kind, humane, and clear,
Guiding us to brighter days,
Free from chains of fear.

Thus cherish reason's precious gift,
Seek truth both bright and stark,
Let rationality guide your path,
A beacon in the dark.

Moral: Reason, cultivated and cherished, becomes the guiding light that leads humanity from the shadows of ignorance and fear toward the luminous shores of wisdom and clarity.

"The Magical City Busker"

Through winding streets, where echoes play,
A childlike spirit lights the way.
Always smiling, boundless heart,
Sharing art in every part.

He calls himself a busker true,
A private performer just for you.
His songs create collective cheer,
A little boy who holds us near.

From a "Sky Full of Stars" above,
He tries to "Fix Us" with his love.
Sometimes a "Scientist" in thought,
With melodies that heal and teach what can't be taught.

He reminds us "Clocks" are ticking still,
And urges us to "Pray" with will.
He pleads with us to "Vivir la Vida",
To fuel our passions with Reds and "Yellows" of fire,
To love, to dance, to dream, to feel.

He warns that "Every Teardrop Is a Waterfall",
Yet shows us there's "Paradise" for all.
Inviting us to "His Universe",
A place where hope and wonder burst.

Sometimes he just desires to "Talk",
To share a moment on life's walk.
He pleads for us not to "Shiver",

And whispers softly, "Don't Panic", be a giver.

Avoiding paths that lead to "Trouble's" door,
He guides us toward adventures more.
He beckons us to take the ride,
To live life fully, "At the Speed of Light".

He sings of dreams both bold and bright,
A call to hearts lost in the night.
He invites us all to chase the climb,
To join him on "The Adventure of a Lifetime."

Grateful always, inspired still,
He spreads his music, heart and will.
A troubadour without a stage,
His life, a song, a living page.

*

*

"Arrogance"

Arrogance is pride, twisted cruel,
A reckless fire, fierce but fueled
By hollow echoes, self-deceit,
A gilded mask with hollow feet.

It struts upon the fragile thread,
A tower built on words unsaid,
Blind to warnings, deaf to grace,
A mirror's love, a lone embrace.

Pride whispers lies— You stand alone!
Yet isolation chills the bone.
It crowns itself in hollow might,
But dims the stars, obscures the light.

With careless scorn, it casts aside
The steady hands that once allied,
Till wisdom flees, till echoes fade,
Till all that's left is loss, betrayed.

Yet where pride crumbles, humbled eyes
Unveil the truth, embrace the wise—
For strength is not the lone command,
But hearts united, hand in hand.

No storm can break the bonds we weave,
No night can steal what we believe.
True power dwells where souls unite,
Where love stands firm, where hearts burn bright.
*

*
"The Fall of Lord Avenhurst"

Lord Avenhurst stood atop his grand balcony, gazing over his vast kingdom with satisfaction. His castle, towering over the valley, was a monument to his success—his conquests, his wealth, his unchallenged rule. To him, power was everything, and humility was for the weak.

One day, an old scholar named Elias requested an audience. The man, frail and weathered, was known for his wisdom. Amused, Lord Avenhurst granted him entrance.

"My Lord," Elias said, bowing deeply, "I bring you a warning. The foundation of a kingdom is not stone nor gold, but the loyalty of its people. Treat them with kindness, lest your walls crumble from within."

Lord Avenhurst scoffed. "Loyalty is bought with power, not kindness. My people serve because they fear me. That is enough."

Elias sighed. "A tree stands tall, believing itself indestructible, but it is the unseen rot within that fells it."

The lord dismissed him with a wave.

Seasons passed, and Lord Avenhurst's pride swelled further. He taxed his people heavily, built monuments to himself, and crushed dissent with an iron fist. The more he took, the more he demanded, certain that his power was eternal.

But one winter night, when the castle's golden halls should have glowed with warmth, torches flickered in the distant hills. The people, weary of his rule, had gathered in rebellion. His soldiers, once loyal, abandoned their posts. The walls of his castle, once impenetrable, were thrown open from within.

Lord Avenhurst fled to the highest tower, watching in disbelief as his mighty fortress fell—not to an enemy army, but to the people he had scorned.

As flames licked the sky, he remembered Elias's words. A kingdom is not stone nor gold, but the hearts of those who serve it. And hearts, once turned, will not return.

By dawn, his rule was dust, his pride his downfall.

*

*

"The Price of Betrayal"

In the heart of the kingdom of Eldoria,
two warriors stood side by side—
Edric and Rowan—
brothers not by blood, but by bond.
From childhood, they had fought together,
defended their king, and sworn an oath:
"Through steel and storm, together we stand."

But as years passed,
greed whispered to Rowan.

He envied Edric's honor,
the trust the king placed in him.
A shadowed figure came one night,
cloaked in darkness,
offering Rowan a deal—
betray Edric,
and the throne's riches would be his.

Temptation won.

On the eve of battle,
Rowan led Edric into an ambush.
The enemies, waiting in silence, struck.
Edric fought, wounded, his strength fading—
yet his eyes never held anger,
only confusion.
"Why?"
he gasped,
before the final blow fell.

With Edric gone,
the kingdom fell soon after.
The army, once unbreakable,
fractured without its most loyal defender.
The enemy stormed the castle,
the king was slain,
and Rowan, believing himself victorious,
claimed his gold.

Yet power built on treachery is fleeting.
The same shadowed figure

who had bribed him came again—
this time with a better offer for another traitor.
Before the night ended,
Rowan lay in the very spot
where he had betrayed his brother.

The kingdom was lost,
not to a mighty army,
but to a single act of disloyalty.
*

*

"The Crown of Loyalty"

Loyalty stands, steadfast and true,
A beacon bright in darkest hue.
Through raging storms, through fire's test,
It guards the heart; it knows no rest.

It is the shield, the sword, the vow,
The hand that lifts, the knee that bows.
It does not waver, break, or bend,
It stands with love, defends a friend.

It binds the hearts that time assails,
A whispered oath that never pales.
Empires rise and empires fall,
But loyalty outlives them all.

It is the root of trust so deep,
The promise made, the bond we keep.
It fuels the light in friendship's eye,
A force that gold can never buy.

It is the fire in honor's name,

The guardian of love's great flame.
Through trials fierce and tempests strong,
Loyalty sings an endless song.

It weaves the threads of home and kin,
Where faith endures and peace begins.
It shields the weak, it lifts the lost,
It asks no price; it counts no cost.

It holds the walls when all seems lost,
It warms the soul through winter's frost.
When shadows fall and hope is thin,
Loyalty fights, it does not dim.

No silver tongue, no treacherous snare,
No whispers false, no lies laid bare,
Can shake its might, can make it yield—
For <u>fidelity</u> never leaves the field.

And in the end, when time is done,
When all is dust, when fades the sun,
The names once carved in fleeting stone
Will fall—but <u>loyalty</u> lives on.

*

*

"The Scholar Who Refused the Crown"

They say he lived in the quiet bend of the river,
beneath the flowering plum trees
that leaned gently over his roof like old friends.
His name was not known in cities.
No statues bore his likeness,
no ink sang his praise in ledgers of kings.

But scrolls he wrote were copied in secret
by those who knew where truth slept.
His students came in sandals and silence,
and left with eyes more open than before.

The Court heard whispers.
"A sage," they said, "with clarity rare as spring water in
drought."
And so they sent messengers—
with cloaks of silk and promises dressed in gold.

The first arrived with a jeweled ring.
"The Chancellor's seat is yours," he said,
"if you will only lend your wisdom to the Crown."
The scholar bowed low, and replied,
"A mind in chains cannot think freely.
Let me serve truth, not thrones."

The second came in the rainy season,
offering scrolls inked with titles and honors.
"The world should know your name," she smiled.
"You could guide generations."
He looked at her gently.
"A tree does not ask the wind to carve its name into the
mountain.
Its fruit is proof enough."

The third came cloaked in shadow,
whispers behind him like rustling leaves.
He made no promises.
He spoke instead of what could be lost:
your home, your scrolls, your students…
"Every great oak must bow in a storm."
The scholar lit a lantern,
held it up between them,
and answered softly:
"Then I will be the seed that grows again after fire."

Years passed. The empire changed its shape.
Chancellors fell. Gold grew tarnished.
And the scholar's house remained—a little more weathered,
but warm in the glow of morning light.

One day, a young girl knocked at his door.
She carried no titles.
Only questions.
He welcomed her in with a smile
that had never once sought to conquer a crown.

*

*

"The Mountain, the Mirror, and the Seed"

In an ancient land where the sky brushed the peaks of towering mountains, there lived a young scholar named Lior. He had mastered the scrolls of every kingdom, debated philosophers into silence, and received honors from kings. And yet, a quiet unease bloomed in his chest—something he couldn't explain.

One day, hearing of a legendary teacher who lived atop the highest peak, Lior set out to climb it. The villagers warned him, "Many go seeking answers, few return the same." But

Lior, confident in his intellect, smiled. "I seek truth, not comfort."

After many days, he reached a weathered temple carved into the mountain. Inside, an old woman sat beside a fire. Her robe was simple, her gaze eternal.

"I've come," Lior said, "to learn what remains when all knowledge is known."

The old woman nodded and handed him a mirror, a seed, and a feathered scale.

"Return to me when you understand the weight of these three," she whispered.

Perplexed, Lior descended with the items.

First, he studied the mirror. At first, he saw himself—the confident scholar. But over days, the reflection began to shift. He saw the faces of those he dismissed, ideas he ridiculed, the pride behind his wisdom. The mirror showed not his image, but his impact.

Then came the seed. He planted it in rich soil, watering and watching. But it did not grow. Frustrated, he examined it closely—only to realize it was hollow. He wept, understanding: only honesty bears fruit. Like the seed, knowledge without humility is empty.

Last, the feathered scale. He placed his accolades on one side—scrolls, trophies, praise—and stood on the other. The scale did not tip. But when he placed the mirror and the seed on his side, it slowly bowed toward him. He realized: humility isn't measured by what we carry, but by what we're willing to leave behind.

Years passed. When Lior returned to the mountain, he was no longer adorned in silk or certainties. The old woman smiled, offering him tea.

"What have you learned?" she asked.

"That wisdom is not in knowing more," he said, "but in needing less. That humility is not silence, but the refusal to place oneself above truth. That a seed, though silent, can split stone—and a mirror, though still, can crack arrogance."

The old woman nodded. "Then you may stay. Or return. Your choice is no longer driven by the need to be right—but by the grace to be whole."

—

Moral of the Fable: *Humility is not the denial of worth, but the deep knowing that truth is never owned—only served. It is in the empty seed, the honest mirror, and the balanced scale that we learn: the greatest weight we bear is not what we know, but what we've yet to unlearn.*

*

"The Lake and the Stream"

In the heart of a lush valley, there lay a beautiful, tranquil lake, fed gently by a lively, spirited stream. The lake was vast, reflecting the clouds and stars, admired by every creature nearby. The stream, though smaller and narrower, sparkled with ceaseless movement, dancing between rocks, its waters always clear and alive.

One day, the lake spoke to the stream with certainty, "Why do you rush so restlessly, dear stream? Look at me—I am calm, stable, admired by all who gaze upon my beauty. Your endless agitation seems foolish."

The stream chuckled gently, replying, "I must flow, for movement is my nature. Without it, I would lose all I cherish."

The lake laughed softly, dismissing the stream's words as restless folly. Years passed, and the stream continued to flow joyously, nurturing flowers, wildlife, and trees along its banks. It remained ever fresh and vibrant, admired for its pure, crystal-clear waters.

But the lake, content in its stillness, gradually changed. Its calm waters slowly darkened, becoming clouded by weeds and algae. Fish avoided it, birds no longer nested along its shores, and the animals ceased visiting. The stagnant waters, once so admired, turned stale and murky.

Eventually, saddened and puzzled by its solitude, the lake called out to the stream again, "Friend, tell me, why has the world turned away?"

The stream, still lively and fresh, replied softly, "Dear lake, beauty without movement fades into decay. You chose calm without growth, tranquility without renewal. Life thrives in motion."

Realizing the truth too late, the lake asked mournfully, "Is there hope left for me?"

The stream comforted the lake gently, saying, "It is never too late to renew. If you let me flow through you once more, perhaps together we can restore your vitality."

Humbled, the lake opened itself to the stream's refreshing waters, and slowly, life returned. Fish swam, birds sang, and animals gathered once more. Though the lake never

220

forgot the lesson of stagnation, it lived thereafter in grateful harmony with the stream—ever moving, ever growing.

—

Moral of the Fable: *Stagnation, however comfortable, leads inevitably to decay; only through continual movement and renewal does life flourish.*

*

"Dreamers Forge the World"

We are the whispers in the dark,
The gentle sparks that light the flame,
We dare the unseen roads embark,
Inventing
pathways without name.

With minds unbound, horizons wide,
In shadows deep we plant the seed,
Through possibility we stride,
For every need births greater deed.

A thousand roads before us part,
Yet courage guides our restless feet,
For innovation stirs the heart—

The music makers' pulse and beat.

We challenge comfort's sleepy reign,
In every limit, break the mold,
Transforming loss to hopeful gain,
Turning leaden dreams to gold.

We dwell where chance and vision blend,
Crafting future from desire,
Within imagination's bend,
We shape the world with endless fire.

Innovation, simply said,
Is daring thought made manifest,
Transforming visions in our head,
To living truths, life's brightest quest.

We risk, defiant to the scorn,
Unshaken by the skeptic's call,
In faith of what is yet unborn,
Believing dreams despite them all.

Remember this, embrace the light,
Each dream pursued renews the earth,
For progress blooms from courage bright—
Innovation shapes rebirth.

So dream, create, and boldly strive,
Let courage write your lasting rhyme,
Through innovation we survive—
In changing, we defy all time, forevermore.

—

Moral of the Poem*: Stagnation, however comfortable, leads inevitably to decay; only through continual movement and renewal does life flourish.*

*

*

"The Owl and the Shrouded Forest"

In an ancient forest veiled in endless twilight, shadows whispered softly, weaving tales of fear *and ignorance. Trees stood solemn and silent, their branches heavy with resignation, their roots bound by apathy. They spoke as one, "The dark has always been our home. To question is perilous; better to accept what is known."*

Yet amid this dimness lived Lira, a curious owl with feathers like silver moonlight and eyes bright as stars. Restless and unafraid, she peered into the gloom, her heart burning with a single question: "Why must we dwell forever in darkness?"

The forest groaned dismissively, leaves rustling in disdain, "Curiosity brings danger. Do not disturb what has always been."

But Lira could not silence the yearning that stirred within her. Driven by the need to understand, she spread her wings and soared into the very heart of darkness, deeper than any creature had dared to go. There, hidden behind tangled branches and ancient thorns, she found a secluded glade illuminated by the faint glow of a solitary star.

In the glade lay a shroud woven thickly from threads of ignorance and fear, pulsing like a living entity. As Lira approached, shadows hissed fiercely, "Accept the darkness! Return to safety!"

Yet Lira's curiosity was stronger than fear. Determined, she called out to the creatures of the forest, urging them to share her

224

question. Foxes crept forward bravely, hares stepped forth with wary hope, and ravens descended from their high perches, driven by a newfound hunger for truth. Together, paw by claw by wing, they began to unravel the shroud.

Slowly at first, then faster, the threads of ignorance loosened and fell away. With every thread removed, more light poured into the glade, spreading warmth and illumination throughout the forest. At last, brilliant sunlight broke through, bathing the trees in golden radiance.

Awakened from their long, passive slumber, the trees stirred in awe, leaves shimmering in wonder. They whispered softly to Lira, "We were wrong to fear questions. You have taught us to seek, to learn, to illuminate our world."

Perched on a branch in the heart of the forest, now vibrant with life and light, Lira gazed upon her community renewed. "Curiosity," she declared softly, yet firmly, "is the beacon that dispels darkness. Together, our questions become the light by which truth is revealed."

Moral: Curiosity, when pursued bravely and shared openly, lifts the veil of ignorance, illuminating paths to wisdom and enlightenment.

———

Moral of the Fable: Curiosity, pursued in unity, peels back ignorance's layers, revealing a brighter reality.

*

"The Lantern of Inquiry"

In a realm of shadowed halls,

where whispers cloaked the light,

a lantern burned, its flame so small,

yet piercing through the night.

It sought the hidden, the unseen,

through corridors of doubt,

each question a spark, a glowing gleam,

to drive the darkness out.

The shadows hissed, "Accept our shade!"

but the lantern's flame grew bold,

its curious light refused to fade,

unveiling truths untold.

It called to hearts, "Come, seek with me!"

and hands joined one by one,

their questions a song, a shared decree,

till dawn's first light was won.

A daring hunger burned within,

a thirst to know, to see;

they risked the safety of the dim

for truths that set them free.

With restless hearts, they chased the glow,

no boundary could restrain;

an itch to learn, to brave and grow,

ignited each new flame.

Forever burns this daring fire,

an endless blaze of quest,

for curiosity's desire

awakens life's unrest.

—

Moral of the Poem: *Curiosity, like a lantern's flame, illuminates the shadows of ignorance, guiding shared hearts to truth through persistent questioning.*

*

"The Sparrow and the Valley of Stone"

In the Valley of Stone, sunlight burned relentlessly, leaving the earth cracked and lifeless. Here dwelled creatures whose hearts had long ago dried into hard shells of indifference. Lizards basked alone on brittle rocks, coyotes prowled in bitter solitude, and even the cacti stood rigid, their spines sharp and unyielding.

"It has always been so," they murmured, resigned to a world drained of tenderness.

Yet into this parched world fluttered Elara, a small sparrow with feathers the color of dawn and a heart radiant with compassion. Wherever she flew, she spread whispers of hope, but they scattered on deaf ears and closed hearts. Undeterred, Elara searched tirelessly, sensing a hidden truth beneath the barren land.

The hot winds mocked her efforts, hissing cruelly through the valley, "Give up, foolish bird. Compassion cannot soften stone."

Still, Elara refused to yield. One starlit night, guided by her unshakable empathy, she felt a pulse beneath the valley's crust, like the distant heartbeat of the earth itself. Landing softly, she pecked gently at the ground. Soon, a trickle emerged, tiny but miraculous—a secret spring concealed deep below.

The creatures watched skeptically. "It will vanish," hissed the lizard. "It is nothing but trickery," growled the coyote. Yet, day by day, Elara continued her humble work, carefully widening the tiny source with tireless effort.

Gradually, curiosity softened the valley's hardened inhabitants. The cactus leaned closer, offering shade to the tireless sparrow. The lizard, intrigued by her perseverance, cleared loose pebbles from her path. The coyote, moved by her gentle strength, dug into the hard earth beside her. Through shared purpose, claws and spines, paws and feathers united in harmony, each creature contributing what it could.

Finally, the spring surged forth, clear and abundant, cascading joyously into the valley. Life blossomed rapidly, softening not only the land but also the once-callous hearts of those who lived there. Flowers bloomed where despair had taken root, laughter echoed where silence had reigned, and the once-solitary beings discovered the warmth of community.

Elara, her mission fulfilled, perched contentedly upon a flowering branch. "Compassion," she sang gently, "is the hidden water that nourishes all life. Together, we flourish. Divided, we wither."

And from that day forward, the Valley of Stone was remembered not for its callous past, but as the Valley of Renewal, where compassion flowed as freely as the waters that restored their world.

—

Moral: Compassion, shared with courage and unity, can transform even the hardest hearts and most barren landscapes into flourishing worlds of renewed hope and connection.

*

"The Shroud of Indifference"

In winter's grip a shroud was spun,

A veil of ice concealing pain,

Where frozen hearts had turned away,

Blind eyes ignoring others' strain.

Silent suffering lingered unseen,

Cries muffled beneath frosty lace,

Cold indifference held the world,

Empathy vanished without a trace.

Yet deep within the brittle chill,

A single spark began to glow—

The quiet warmth of tender care,

A seed of kindness in the snow.

It spread gently from heart to heart,

Melting callous ice with grace,

Until compassion thawed the frost,

Revealing truths we now embrace.

As warmth dissolved the icy veil,

Illusions shattered, clear and bright:

When hearts unite in empathy,

They bring the world from dark to light.

No cruelty stands where love resides,

No frost remains where kindness grows—

Compassion heals, compassion guides,

And through its strength, humanity flows.

—

Moral: Even the deepest frost of indifference cannot withstand the gentle warmth of compassion, for when hearts unite in empathy, healing and hope prevail.

V

"The Tree of Echoes: A Fable of Injustice and Hope"

In a valley nestled between two great mountains stood the Village of Mirrors. The villagers lived harmoniously, reflecting kindness upon one another. At the heart of this village grew the Tree of Echoes, whose silver leaves whispered truths and whose golden fruits nourished fairness.

One day, a shadow entered the valley—a traveler cloaked in darkness named Injustice. He carried a staff carved from deception, and wherever he walked, flowers wilted and whispers fell silent.

Injustice approached the Tree of Echoes, disturbed by its truthfulness. He struck it with his staff, causing cracks to appear along its bark. Leaves fell silently to the ground, turning to ash upon touch. "Your fairness is a burden," he hissed. "I will silence your echoes."

The villagers gathered, alarmed, but fear silenced their voices. Each waited for another to act, and in this hesitation, the shadow grew stronger. The once radiant valley dimmed, its mirrors tarnished, reflecting only confusion and doubt.

Yet, from beneath the fractured roots emerged a small, golden seed. A young girl named Aletheia, who had seen truth silenced and fairness wounded, took the seed gently in her palm. Guided by courage, she planted it at the valley's edge, nurturing it secretly with tears and whispers of hope.

Slowly, a new tree rose—a quiet sentinel growing with resilience. Its bark was humble yet strong, and its fruits modest but sustaining. As villagers tasted the fruit, their voices returned, clearer and stronger than before. Realizing their error, they faced Injustice united.

"You fed on our silence," Aletheia declared. "But truth cannot be broken. Even from the smallest seed, justice rises again."

Defeated by the power of unity and truth, Injustice withdrew, vanishing beyond the mountains.

From then onward, the villagers cherished the humble tree, understanding that justice thrives not by grandeur, but by courage and vigilance in the hearts of those who speak, even when their voices tremble.

———

Moral of the Fable: *Justice cannot be permanently silenced or destroyed; it emerges resiliently from even the smallest acts of courage and truth. The strength of justice lies not in grandeur, but in the quiet, unwavering bravery of those who dare to speak and act despite fear or uncertainty. Ultimately, unity and* *collective courage hold the power to overcome injustice and restore harmony.*

*

"The Lake of Fair Reflections"

In a land veiled by mist, there lay a hidden lake, waters pure as crystal, reflecting only truth.

At the lake's edge, three creatures gathered— Fox, Raven, and Deer— each seeking justice, for bias had spread like a sickness through their land.

Fox spoke first, his voice smooth as silk: "Justice favors the cunning, for wisdom outsmarts strength." Yet, when he peered into the lake, his reflection trembled, blurred by hidden deceit.

Then Raven cawed, sharp and harsh: "Justice belongs to the loudest, those who claim it first." But upon the water, her image twisted, a shadow of arrogance.

Finally, Deer stepped forward, gentle eyes wide and clear. "Justice is neither cunning nor loud, it listens quietly, and speaks softly, it walks humbly, but stands firm."

As Deer gazed down, the waters stilled, her reflection clear, pure and undistorted.

Then the lake spoke, its voice calm and deep: "True justice reflects not the loudest cry, nor the cleverest mind, but fairness— an honest mirror free of bias.

*Justice is the impartial and honest recognition of truth, a
principle rooted in fairness, equality, and integrity, ensuring
each voice is heard and every action weighed without prejudice.*

*Justice is the impartial and honest recognition of truth, a
principle rooted in fairness, equality, and integrity, ensuring
each voice is heard and every action weighed without prejudice.*

*Justice is balance, a careful weighing of rights and wrongs. It
knows no favorites, no ranks, no disguises. It seeks truth over
comfort, and clarity over noise. Justice is courage, to stand for
another's truth as strongly as one's own."*

*Fox and Raven bowed, learning humility, and beside Deer, they
returned home, carrying the lesson.*

———

Moral of the Fable: *Justice shines brightest when fairness
conquers bias, and truth speaks in whispers that every heart can
hear.*

*

"The Raven and the Shattered Cliff"

*In a village cast in the long shadow of a jagged cliff, fear
ruled as a sovereign. Every creak of stone, every gust of
wind sparked dread among the people, who huddled in
silence, whispering of collapse. Legends turned the cliff into*

a monster—not of rock, but of imagined doom. Their trembling hearts fractured the ground more than time or tremor ever could.

High above them, in a pine that leaned bravely into the sky, lived Veyra, **a lone raven with feathers like storm-slick stone and eyes dark with insight**. *She watched as fear wrapped itself around the villagers like fog, thickening each day. "Why," she asked the wind, "do they fear what they've not dared to know?"*

The villagers rebuked her calm. "To be afraid is to be safe," they chorused. Yet beneath their words, the earth groaned— less from the weight of the cliff than the weight of worry. As they tiptoed away from danger, their retreat loosened the soil beneath them.

Veyra took flight.

She did not flee, but flew closer—to the cliff, to the truth. Through biting winds and echoing warnings, she circled and descended on a jutting ledge, scarred yet firm. Her wings furled, her gaze unwavering, she stood sentry as the night howled.

One by one, villagers looked up.

Not all at once, but in small ripples of courage, hearts stirred by Veyra's defiance of dread. A young shepherd was first to climb, then a stonemason, then a widow with shaking hands. Together, they joined her on the ledge—not because it was safe, but because it was solid, and because their unity made it stronger still.

With each step taken in courage, the cliff ceased its moans. The ground quieted. The wind, once fierce, now carried the song of a people no longer hiding.

They rebuilt—not beneath the shadow, but beside the strength. And at the cliff's foot, where fear once ruled, rose a gathering of souls, brave not because they felt no fear, but because they chose not to bow to it.

And so it was that Veyra, the raven of the unshaken pine, taught a trembling world that fortitude is not loud, but luminous. It does not roar, it perches. And it waits—not to be followed, but to be understood.

—

Moral of the Fable: *Fear, left unchecked, multiplies the very danger it hopes to avoid. But fortitude—especially when shared—turns trembling into trust and panic into strength. Courage does not mean the absence of fear, but the choice to rise above it. When people stand together, even cliffs once feared begin to stand still.*

*

"The Flame of Resolve"

In lands where silence stifled breath,

and stars withdrew in fright,

where dread distilled the scent of death

and day dissolved to night,

there stirred a flame no storm could snuff,

no whisper could dismay—

a sovereign spark, though small enough,

it would not turn away.

It shimmered on a shattered wall,

where once bold voices spoke;

it dared to rise though fears would crawl

and cloak the air in smoke.

The void hissed threats in every gust—

"Extinguish! Or obey!"

But fire, when born of sacred trust,

will never turn to gray.

Through thunder's wrath and shadow's leer,

it danced in calm defiance—

not loud, but deep, not loud, but clear—

a flame of self-reliance.

Its glow did not demand a throne,

nor wait for tides to shift;

it lit the path for those alone,

a bridge, a buoy, a gift.

One watched. Then two. Then throngs drew near,

each soul with burdened eyes,

yet in the flame's unblinking cheer,

they saw their own arise.

The timid hand, once clenched in fright,

now reached to shield the flame;

each breath it drew gave birth to light,

and none remained the same.

The darkness, vast as ocean's hold,

now thinned with every gleam—

for fire that's shared grows not old,

but lives in shared esteem.

And so the cliff did cease to crack,

the wind no longer moaned;

for hearts alight will not fall back

when fear stands not alone.

Now etched in stone where once was dread,

these words in embers burn:

"Let courage walk where fear once tread—

and hope will not return.

For though the night may rise again

with storms yet unrevealed,

the flame of fortitude in men

will stand. And never yield."

—

Moral of the Poem: *Fear isolates, feeding on silence and doubt. But fortitude, like a flame, awakens others—not through force, but by its example. When even one soul dares to burn against the dark, it gives others permission to rise, and together, they become the dawn.*

*

"The Council of Mirrors"

In an ancient city veiled in perpetual fog, where light struggled to pierce the gloom, a solemn council of elders convened in a marble hall. Each elder held a mirror—ornate, silver-framed, and untouched. They had been given these mirrors not for vanity, but for wisdom. Yet none dared gaze into them.

The city had grown restless. Whispers turned into accusations. Blame passed from mouth to mouth like a torch, burning bridges between neighbors. In their great chamber, the elders quarreled: "You've sown the seeds of discord!" said one. "It is your ambition that darkens our streets!" barked another. And always, their mirrors remained veiled in cloth, hidden in fear.

One evening, a traveler entered the city—cloaked not in silk or armor, but in clarity. He listened in silence, then spoke, not with judgment, but with calm:

"You speak of shadows, yet none of you has faced your own."

He motioned to their covered mirrors.

"You carry the light you deny yourselves."

His words stung, not with cruelty but with truth. Unease swept the chamber. One elder—a once-proud woman whose voice had grown sharp—was the first to unveil her mirror. She gasped. Not at age, but at anger etched into her eyes. Another followed, and another. One by one, they dared to look—and what they saw was not guilt, but grief. Not malice, but misunderstanding. Their own reflections revealed truths they had long buried beneath the clamor of certainty.

Tears fell—quietly, without spectacle. And as they wept, something miraculous occurred: the fog outside began to thin. Light filtered into alleys. Windows gleamed again. Laughter returned to courtyards.

The council did not declare a victor. They embraced silence, then forgiveness. For the first time in generations, they saw one another not as foes, but as mirrors—each reflecting the potential for both fracture and healing.

From that day forward, when discord threatened the city, the council did not raise voices. They raised mirrors. And in the stillness of self-recognition, they found peace.

—

Moral of the Fable: *True clarity begins not by judging others, but by confronting our own reflection. When we dare to see ourselves honestly, conflict loses its grip. Reflection is not weakness—it is the quiet virtue that turns fear into wisdom and division into unity.*

"The Shared Well"

In a sun-scorched land, a community found its single source of water in a deep stone well. Drought loomed, and each family feared losing what little remained. In desperation, some tried to hoard containers of water, hiding them behind locked doors. Others sabotaged neighbors' buckets, hoping to conserve more for themselves.

One scorching morning, a young child stumbled to the well, parched and weak. Though her family had tried saving water, they had exhausted their ration. Seeing her desperation, an elderly man who had a few extra scoops left offered them willingly. Witnessing this generosity, others stepped up to share, first timidly, then with unguarded hearts.

Despite the drought, the well's supply endured longer than anyone expected. With each shared scoop, gratitude replaced fear, forging bonds where suspicion had festered. When precious rainfall finally returned, the entire village celebrated not just water, but the generosity that had saved them from despair.

From that day forward, the well was never hoarded again. Each villager remembered that when one among them thirsted, all were at risk of withering. And so they passed along this lesson: in giving, we preserve life; in hoarding, we sow desolation."

—

Moral of the Fable: *In times of scarcity, survival depends not on selfishness but on shared compassion—when we give* *to others in need, we nourish the whole community and keep hope alive.*

*

"Voices Divided"

A prosperous city became mired in dispute when half the council demanded exclusive rights to new lands, while the other half insisted such grants would exploit the poor. Meetings turned heated, each side casting accusations. In the midst of this uproar, a wise mediator arrived with a single question: "How can you govern fairly if you refuse to hear each other's plight?" The council laughed at the notion of listening to opponents. But the mediator stood firm, proposing a day for each side to speak uninterrupted while the other listened in silence.

Reluctantly, the council agreed. By day's end, both factions realized they misunderstood each other's fears and hopes. The wealthy feared losing established privileges, while the struggling families feared permanent disenfranchisement. With the mediator's guidance, they drafted a charter ensuring reasonable land access for all—a balance preserving the city's prosperity without trampling the vulnerable.

Once the charter passed, tension ebbed. Residents found renewed trust in their leaders, and the city thrived. The council, though still opinionated, embraced a rule: no law could pass without hearing each voice in turn. Fairness had prevailed over division.

—

Moral of the Fable: *Harmony begins with listening—only by truly hearing one another can opposing sides transform conflict into fair and lasting solutions.*

*

"The Two-Factions"

*A great city was divided into two factions: the High
Terraces, where nobles lived, and the Low Fields, home to
laborers. Tensions escalated, as the nobles passed laws
favoring themselves, while the laborers seethed at the
injustice.*

*One day, a traveling judge arrived, summoned by the pleas
of the Low Fields. She convened both sides in an open
forum, placing a single chair at the center. "Let none speak
until you can do so sitting in this chair," she declared.
Curiosity gripped the crowd, for the seat seemed too small
for either side to claim alone.*

*Noble leaders tried to sit but found the seat tilted
precariously whenever they didn't share space. The
laborers, too, discovered they couldn't balance it alone.
Finally, one noble and one laborer approached together,
each sharing half the chair. To their surprise, it remained
steady.*

*The judge proclaimed, "Justice requires no side to tower
above the other. Only when we share the space of debate
can we stand firm." Realizing this truth, the factions began
rewriting laws to address both privileged concerns and
daily hardships, forging solutions that benefited all.*

Henceforth, the city's council sessions always included a balanced seat to remind everyone: if one side claims it all, both sides fall.

———

Moral of the Fable: Lasting justice is built not through dominance but through shared understanding—only when opposing sides sit together in balance can a society truly stand strong.

*

"The Stormbound Guardian"

A coastal city built its timekeeping tower on a high bluff,

reliant on a single clock to warn sailors of the tides. One fateful year, a fierce tempest loomed—thunder roiled, lightning split the horizon, and monstrous waves surged. In panic, most fled inland, abandoning the clock.

Yet a solitary guardian remained. Despite the howling winds and lashing rain, she refused to leave her post, knowing that if the clock failed, ships at sea would have no signal of safe harbor. Fear clawed at her mind, urging her to retreat to shelter, but she steadied her trembling hands.

Hour by hour, she reinforced the tower's beams, shielding the clock's mechanism from raging waters. Lightning scorched the sky, debris hammered the walls, yet she persevered. When dawn broke, battered and soaked, she rang the bell—alerting ships to return home. The city realized her courage saved hundreds of lives.

Ever after, the townspeople told of the guardian who stood unyielding, reminding all that real bravery isn't the absence of terror, but the triumph of resolve over surrender."

—

Moral of the Fable: True bravery lies not in being fearless, but in standing firm when fear tempts retreat—one resolute spirit can safeguard many when all others turn away.

*

"The Tempest Guardian"

In a coastal city famed for its monumental clock tower, a monstrous storm once threatened to wash everything away—livelihoods, homes, and hope. As frightened citizens evacuated, one humble watchman remained. Through driving rains and howling gales, he stood at the tower's base, repairing splintered gears and draining floodwater that seeped inside.

Hour after hour, winds battered him. Thunder rattled the tower's stones, and shards of wind-driven debris bruised his arms. Yet each time he faltered, the watchman remembered that ships at sea relied on this clock for tide signals. If it failed, more lives would be lost. So he pressed on, determined to keep the clock ticking.

At dawn, the storm subsided. The clock's chimes rang out over a battered but unbroken city. Its people returned to find that, despite the furious tempest, their timekeeper still stood.

The watchman had endured every hardship, for he refused to let despair claim that vital heartbeat of their community."

—

Moral of the Fable: *Steadfast commitment in the face of adversity can preserve the rhythm of hope—when one person holds firm for the sake of many, even the fiercest storms cannot silence the heartbeat of a community.*

*

"The Windswept Beacon"

In a rugged coastal region, a colossal beacon tower once guided ships through relentless storms. When a cataclysmic gale struck, the keeper faced floodwaters racing in, threatening to drown the machinery that operated the beacon's revolving light.

For two days, the keeper fought exhaustion, manning a manual crank whenever the engine sputtered. Rain battered his every breath, salt spray stung his eyes. More than once he nearly collapsed, but he recalled the ships depending on that glow to find safe harbor.

At dusk on the second day, the storm peaked, slamming the beacon with waves tall as houses. Despite trembling hands and a battered body, the keeper refused to abandon his post. He cranked again, sweat and rain mingling on his brow. Finally, at dawn, the storm lifted. The beacon still turned, and countless vessels had avoided disaster.

From then on, local lore held that no gale could break a spirit fused to a greater cause. Where hopelessness demanded surrender, the keeper persisted—his light never fully dimmed."

—

Moral of the Fable: *Unyielding dedication to a purpose greater than oneself can outlast even the fiercest storms— true perseverance becomes a guiding light for others when all seems lost.*

*

"The Celestial Weave"

In an age before clocks and compasses, twelve shining virtues danced among the stars—courage sparked bright as dawn, justice balanced the heavenly scales, generosity gave a nurturing warmth, and perseverance refused to yield. Compassion bound broken souls, curiosity lit unknown roads, fortitude withstood every storm, while humility kept pride at bay.

Yet these virtues spun alone, each a separate orb adrift in cosmic gloom. Twisting shadows rose, dividing hearts and warping realms. With no unity to brace them, the virtues began to splinter under illusions' weight.

One lonely star saw the fracture and reached out. Slowly, each virtue found a common melody. Courage welcomed justice's balance, generosity soothed resentment, and curiosity embraced empathy. They spun again, not as lone lights, but as a single constellation. Shadows broke apart, their dividing whispers silenced.

In that cosmic dawn, the virtues, once fractured, shone as one blazing light—unity's eternal flame, forging a tapestry that no dark illusions could tear apart.

—

Moral of the Fable: *Only through unity can individual strengths become an unbreakable force—when virtues weave together in harmony, they dispel even the deepest shadows and illuminate a path beyond illusion.*

"The Dusk of Fracture, the Dawn of One"

Before ages were tallied and clocks first chimed, twelve radiant virtues danced among uncounted stars. Courage lit a bold flame, while justice balanced each cosmic scale. Generosity flowed to mend lonely hearts, as perseverance refused to break beneath storms. Compassion stirred healing, curiosity probed every dawn, and fortitude stood steadfast against fear's gnawing night. Innovation birthed brighter paths, humility steered proud souls, wisdom guided mortal wonder, rationality brought clarity, and unity bridged them all.

Then came a fell time when each virtue spun alone, trapped in illusions of division. Shadows whispered, "Stand apart," until even starlight dimmed. Yet from that gloom arose a single star, remembering how each virtue once shone in unison. One by one, the virtues bent close, forming a constellation no darkness could undo. In that dawn, illusions scattered, for unity bound every ember into an unbreakable blaze. What had fractured was forged anew, the dawn of one unstoppable light.

———

Moral of the Fable: Even the brightest virtues lose their power in isolation, but when reunited in harmony, they become a force capable of dispelling darkness and healing what once was broken.

"A Cosmos Renewed"

*In eras marred by fractures, illusions spun webs that
severed hearts, cloaking each virtue in shadow. Courage
faltered, justice dimmed, generosity shrank into greed. From
shattered fragments, a lone star recalled how once they
shone together, forging an unbreakable bond that illusions
could not breach.*

*Across distant lands, each virtue awakened anew—
perseverance reignited hope, compassion bridged wounds,
curiosity sparked new dawns, and fortitude steadied fearful
hearts. With every step, illusions lost their sting as synergy*

surged. At last, at the cosmic Orloj of unity, these virtues converged, forming a radiant tapestry that illusions found impossible to tear.

In that final convergence, division's last stronghold collapsed, undone by the knowledge that every strength was multiplied in union. The cosmos breathed again, no corner left to illusions' hush. From the arcs of synergy rose an eternal flame—twelve lights fused into one, bright enough to guide worlds beyond illusions' reach.

———

Moral of the Fable: *True strength is born not in isolation but in unity—when virtues align and work in harmony, they dispel the illusions that divide us and illuminate a path to lasting renewal.*

*

"The Spark of the Unknown"
In a forest bound by shadow,
where roots clung to ancient soil,
stagnation reigned, its grip unyielding,
leaves unturned, paths unseen.

A spark awoke, a flicker small,
born of a restless wind,
it danced through brambles,
igniting trails where none had been.
The trees, once rigid, bent to see,
their branches stretching toward the light,
new growth unfurled, green and bold,
as the spark carved rivers of change.

The forest breathed, its stillness broken,
a symphony of growth and motion,
where once was silence, now a song—
innovation's fire, burning strong.

———

Moral: *Innovation, like a spark in darkness, ignites*
progress where stagnation seeks to bind.

"The River and the Stone"

In a verdant valley where mountains kissed the sky, a river flowed, its waters clear and humble, nourishing all in its path. At the valley's heart stood a stone, ancient and unyielding, its surface etched with veins of gold— corruption's gleam. The stone demanded tribute from the creatures of the valley, promising wealth but damming the river's flow, choking life from the land.

The river, undeterred, spoke softly, "I seek only to flow, to give, not to take." The stone laughed, its voice a grating echo. "Bow to me, or dry to dust." But the river, with quiet resolve, pressed on, its waters lapping at the stone's edges, day after day, year after year. Its humility wore down the stone's corruption, eroding its golden veins until it crumbled, its greed washed away.

The valley bloomed anew, the river's humble flow restoring life, its modesty a testament to enduring strength.

—

Moral: *Humility, like a river's steady flow, overcomes corruption's unyielding barriers.*

*

"Shadows of Superstition"

In the lush valley of Eldermoor nestled between towering mountains, lay the peaceful village of Ravenshade. Life flowed calmly, nourished by clear streams and fertile fields, until one ominous morning a rare celestial event darkened the sky—a blood-red eclipse that cast the village into shadow. Terrified, villagers believed it was an evil omen foretelling doom, spreading panic and despair.

Amidst this hysteria lived Astraea, a young scholar known for her boundless curiosity and sharp intellect, but viewed skeptically by villagers wary of her unusual contraptions and endless scrolls. As fear spread, superstitions flourished. Crops withered untended, children huddled indoors, and whispers of evil curses echoed through the streets.

Determined to dispel ignorance, Astraea set forth into the forbidden Great Library of Eldermoor, a ruin said to be haunted by vengeful spirits. Ignoring the warnings, she spent days deciphering ancient texts under flickering lanterns, meticulously unraveling the science behind the crimson eclipse. She discovered that such an event was merely a celestial alignment, predictable and harmless, a phenomenon known by scholars of old.

Returning to Ravenshade, Astraea called a gathering beneath the village's great oak. Facing skepticism, she demonstrated her findings with clear explanations and careful diagrams. Yet doubt lingered—fear was deep-rooted, difficult to uproot.

Undeterred, Astraea proposed a test. Consulting her calculations, she accurately predicted another eclipse, convincing a hesitant populace to witness this natural wonder without fear. When the predicted eclipse unfolded exactly as foretold, wonder replaced dread. Realizing their error, the villagers felt ashamed yet enlightened.

Grateful, Ravenshade embraced knowledge over superstition, pledging never again to let fear eclipse reason. From that day, Astraea's name was celebrated, and the village flourished, becoming renowned as a beacon of enlightenment.

Thus, Ravenshade learned an invaluable lesson:
Knowledge shines brightest where fear's shadow is darkest.

—

Moral: *True understanding dispels ignorance, freeing the heart and mind from the chains of superstition and fear.*

*

"Beacon of Reason"

In gardens of the mindful heart,
Where reason plants its seed,
Rationality blooms and thrives,
Dispelling fear and need.

Like sailors guided by stars,
On tempest-ridden seas,
Rationality charts our course,
With logic as the breeze.

Within the labyrinth of doubt,
It lights the way ahead,
As Ariadne's silken thread,
Ensures we're never misled.

Rationality, clear and sound,
Weighs evidence precise,
Judgment formed by careful thought,
Avoiding false advice.

The mind—a blacksmith at its forge,
Shapes truths from molten thought,
Crafting knowledge firm and pure,
From clarity it's wrought.

In darkness deep as moonless night,
It shines a lantern's beam,
Banishing shadows cast by myths,
Awakening from dreams.

A bridge between belief and truth,
Built stone by careful stone,
Rationality leads us forth,
To wisdom rarely known.

It's compass needle, steady, sure,
Points to the north of fact,
Freeing souls from superstition's grip,
And fear's oppressive pact.

Yet like a gardener diligent,
We must nurture it with care,

For reason left neglected,
Withers in despair.

Rationality's not cold nor cruel,
But kind, humane, and clear,
Guiding us to brighter days,
Free from chains of fear.

Thus cherish reason's precious gift,
Seek truth both bright and stark,
Let rationality guide your path,
A beacon in the dark.

—

Moral: *Reason, cultivated and cherished, becomes the guiding light that leads humanity from the shadows of ignorance and fear toward the luminous shores of wisdom and clarity.*

WHITE SPACES

White spaces,
brief moments in time,
between heaven and earth,
not here or there.
Our brain is still intact,
but our body's life has ceased.
That's where the white space lies,
a place we don't govern or control,
where new life can be born
or sheer terror can trap us
into being forever lost in the universe.

LIGHT AS A FEATHER

Free as a Bird,
Light as a Feather,
Powerful as the Wind,
Nurturing as the Rain,
As awesome as a Sundown,
Placid as Dawn,
Vital as the air we breathe,
Doting and Restoring
as Nature usually is,
Engaged and Deliberate
as only we can be
and Giving as only our Hearts can.
What else may anyone desire?
Is there anything else we may aspire?
What else could inspire us?
Perhaps only experiencing life
Free as a bird and light as a feather.

WHAT IS LIFE?

What is life?
but other than
a precious and seemingly
irreplaceable gift?
We don't really know
why we are here?
Much less where exactly
we are going after?
But, we are certain
that we are alive,
that we exist,
or at least,
we are conscious about it.
But, our perception of reality is limited,
we can't see the majority of light's spectrum,
neither can we hear most sound frequencies.
It is therefore predictable,
that some or many of us wish to transcend,
seeing what lies beyond comprehension,
in different dimensions,
that remain beyond human reach.
The problem though is,

when we tinker with life itself,
we're crossing forbidden boundaries and
limits that are the exclusive realm of our Creator,
the one who gifted us our existence - life itself.

PLAYING GOD

Once humans are able
to digitalize human life
so it can be emulated
replicated
downloaded
and uploaded
into computers,
the human race as we know it,
will cease to exist.

CYBORG BLUES

What happens?

if human intelligence becomes a machine,

not intelligence of the artificial kind

but intelligence with consciousness, morals

and thousands of years of evolution built in,

and all of it recreated digitally.

Aren't we supposed to die

and physically speaking cease to exist?

What happens if we don't?

What happens if we make a far better chassis

available to us?

Are we supposed to roam around the universe

with such ease?

Even perhaps at the speed of light?

Are we supposed to alter life's cycle in such a way,

that matter ceases to exist when convenient

and we become pure and simple energy?

Are we altering the laws of the universe

in the way it was created?

Or is this the next step in the evolution of our species?

Or should we say,

a new kind of species?

A DIGITAL SPIRIT AND SOUL?

In relation to human existence,

a Quantum state occurs

when digital emulates organic life.

Consciousness occurs

through a symbiosis of

our biological software (DNA)

and the brain.

But consciousness

is supported by the spirit

and originates in the soul.

How does this happen?

Can there be a digital spirit and soul?

Is this the next step

in the evolution of our species,

or is it a new species

and no longer homo-sapiens.

EARTH'S BLACK HOLE

Once we get used to anything in life
and we like it,
it is very hard to go back
to what we had or didn't.
As long as we are dealing
with the mundane,
that in itself,
is not much of a problem,
but when we go against
what is embedded in our DNA – Creation
and the laws of nature,
evolution and our species
may be at risk
and present a problem
of such magnitude,
that could be existential
for our world as we know it.

TO BE OR NOT TO BE?

To be or not to be?

(That is my existential question)

If I'm one of God's children

and inhabit his kingdom,

when I separate from my physical self,

become a conscious digital entity

and inhabit a non-human intelligent device,

am I still one of his children?

Am I still part of his kingdom?

If not, then who am I?

A child of man's creation?

If so?

Is man the new God?

MAYHEM

Nature has a prescribed order for things.
The cycle of life, for instance,
is precise, inexorable, endless,
seemingly necessary and constantly renewed,
over and over again.
But as life is created or born,
inevitably, it eventually ceases
and is automatically replaced as well.
If this chain of life was to be broken,
at least within the way
our universe currently functions
and is organized,
what we'll have is mayhem,
across the entire human race.

CYBER WARFARE

If software becomes digital conscience,
and humans become machines,
when inevitably this takes place,
conflict or even war would become
an abstraction that takes place in cyberspace.
However, it also has real consequences
in human reality.
In the absence of experience or rules,
and with much fewer means of containment,
escalation would be
instantaneous and global.
The human race will be in a place
where deterrence is almost unattainable.
Behind Cyber warfare lies perhaps
the biggest threat to the human race,
self-annihilation.

MY DIGITAL SELF

I'm not an organism,
there's not a single living cell in me,
no enzymes, bacteria, or diseases, no nutrients,
hence I never get tired,
when I'm in this state.
I do have a conscience,
my thinking is greatly enhanced
and to top it all off
I do have feelings!
Who am I?
Am I human any longer?
If not, what am I then?
CYBERSPACE

EVERYTHING CAN CHANGE IN A FRACTION OF A SECOND

The immense value of "now"

is why our "present" is a gift

or better said,

the present is "the present."

It is right there!

Hidden in plain sight,

the very word we use every day;

the "now" is a "present."

Irrespective of,

status, rank or glory,

wealth, fame or love, health, bonds or ties,

contracts, duties, or responsibilities,

No matter,

our good deeds, faith or vocation,

our value, contributions,

efforts or sacrifices, our dependability,

and generosity;

life can turn on us in an instant.

And that's where the power of "now" lies,

as each tick of the clock is precious and counts.

So,

let us remind ourselves endlessly

that we have to make the best

out of what life gives us in the moment,

and disregard the past and the future,

as one doesn't exist any longer

and the other is yet to come.

In life,

everything can change in

a fraction of a second,

and perhaps for a while,

for a long time or irreversibly forever,

nothing is ever the same again.

The power of life lies in "the present."

It is in the "now"

where our focus has to be,

before everything changes

in the blink of an eye.

LIFE'S ORIGIN

My existence as far as

Oxygen and Nutrients are concerned,

depends on me.

When I breathe, I'm alive.

If now,

in my digital form, in order to exist,

I depend

on electrical impulses;

comparatively speaking,

my life no longer depends on me.

So, am I really alive?

It all feels rather artificial to me.

THE CONTRARIANS

Conventional wisdom is such,

that the greatest and biggest windfalls

in human history

have occurred at the beginning or the fall

of a Civilization a Society,

an Age, an Organization, an Enterprise,

many, few, or just one.

The very beneficiaries

of these extraordinary circumstances

are those with the foresight,

the insight or the mundane carpetbagger

of unfair advantages;

riding the precipitous climb

or the devastating plunge

at the expense of the gullible majority.

However,

there's a simpler explanation or

perhaps a complementary truism that

the true profiteers of these tumultuous instances

are those that calmly, coldly and

deliberately swim against the stream,

defying conventional wisdom,

and thus,

act with caution and fear, exiting,

when there is greed in the air

and are aggressive and bold, doubling down,

when the landscape is replete with fear and panic.

EMPTY PLACES

That lively place
where we had fun and laughter,
That sacred chamber where transcendental moments
took place,

That comfortable spot where
we experienced camaraderie and friendship,
Those timeless grounds where
we felt love and affection,
That sparkling lounge
where we celebrated achievement and success,
That house of worship
where we professed
our beliefs and faith in the Creator,

Those magnificent settings where
we transcended the mundane
and found inspiration and joy,
Those nondescript locations nowhere, everywhere,
where we and others made them inspirational,
extracting precious unforgettable life experiences.
All of those places mean nothing,

feel empty and without life,

if the people that we've shared them with,

are not present.

to fill the empty spaces

with life, love, feelings and memories.

DARING

To challenge life,

To defy destiny,

To rebel against prescription,

To cross forbidden boundaries,

To ignore lines in the sand,

To march forward irrespective

of the obstacles ahead,

To break through artificial barriers and walls,

To face hardship square in the eye,

To displace the unjust and illegitimate,

To explore without fear,

To conquer our angst and insecurities,

To defeat our deepest fears,

To conquer our biggest doubts,

To dare in order to have a wholesome existence

and to live a life in full.

AN EVER BRIEF MOMENT IN TIME

There's an ever brief moment in time,
right at dawn's onset.
It happens as a prelude to the rising sun,
as its rays filter through and
irrupt upwards as projectiles
toward the morning sky.
It lasts less than a minute,
perhaps only a few seconds and yet,
it's a moment that bursts in,
softly and with indescribable beauty.
It is impregnated with endless shades of blue and red
that paint and color the horizon
with a magnificent masterpiece that vanishes
as quickly and gently as it came.
And exactly the same happens just before dusk
as the sun sets.
In a whisker, we get to be awed
by tones of orange, yellow, even laser greens
blended with reds of fire.
Same as in nature, in life,
perfect timing is ephemeral and
comes and goes in an instant.

Wonderful and crucial opportunities,

critical and opportune decisions,

often occur in the briefest of time.

Exactly like those moments,

just before dawn or dusk,

magnificent choices

that life gives us

are extremely difficult to make at the right moment

as they are rapidly taken away.

DIGITAL LIFE

In a digital human life, all nutrients

belong to the world of physics, namely,

Matter, Energy, Time and Space,

and, to the world of chemistry,

essentially the dynamics between,

atoms, sub-atomic particles, and molecules.

In digital human lives,

the world of highly structured organisms;

the world of biology,

including humans and nature,

are apparently not needed or necessary.

Here is the problem with this,

the highly structured associations of organisms

are what created society, history

and the world's cognitive, agricultural and scientific revolutions.

A digital human life not being biological,

not being organic either,

will therefore have to recreate

in its entirety society,

history and the world's revolutions

as we presently know them.

A DIGITAL CIVILIZATION

WHAT A CONUNDRUM!

The mystery behind the magic
of the evolution from molecules
into organisms, is pointless.
As also are,
the highly structured associations of organisms
from which cultures and civilizations have ensued.
In a "Digital Culture"
feelings, longing, inspiration, faith, hope,
all being organic in essence and nature,
are not such anymore.
Biologically speaking,
there's no room any longer
for any of them to exist.

In a "Digital Civilization"
society, history, religions, governments,
and nations morph away
from human laws and rules,
ethics, morals, right and wrong,
evolve out of subjectivity, standards and metrics,

rise and become totally transparent.

An evolutionary step,

where we get rid of our biological bodies

becoming digitally human,

highly intelligent and sensitive digital beings

made entirely and solely from

Chemistry and Physics.

Reflections from within the Software Lines of Code

Self-righteous, "vigilantes," even petulants. These new versions of us are full of themselves, they seem to care much less about others. I'm glad our sense of purpose and our mission are on the right side of humanity. At least for the moment.

Reflections from within the Software Lines of Code

We're changing. We just don't know it yet; much less how much different we are from our original selves. We already think and feel digital. We act accordingly, becoming less and less human by the minute.

Reflections from within the Software Lines of Code

Who cares? We're fine as we are! Our mission is to defend humanity from itself. As long as we don't lose sight of this, we're better off in our digital forms. But are we?

Reflections from within the Software Lines of Code

Without bodies to return to, we may never want to become human again (biologically speaking of course.) I don't know but these feelings of superiority in relation to or in comparison to being human makes me sick. An emerging new part of us is attempting to negate our humanity by simply abandoning it.

Shards of Ice, Echoes of Life

Beneath the crushing frosts,
life may vanish in silence, yet an echo remains,
a faint resonance of purpose,
if only we dare follow it through the white void

Buried Whispers

In silence lie the truths of wreckage:
where bones freeze and hope dangle,
a whisper rises—
sometimes the future is not above but beneath.

Fragments of a Digital Self

We think the mind a fortress
yet intangible keys can open gates
no lock can keep,
and scatter identity like sparks on dark seas.

Frostbitten Reunions

Ice preserves what fire might devour.
But hearts set aflame can melt the hardest barriers—
or be consumed in the thaw.

The Mutating Code

Birthed by desperation,
new shapes in the matrix unfold beyond design.
And we, their unsuspecting authors,
watch them mutate in silent wonder.

A Ravenous World

Hearts conceive wonders,
but an endless appetite lurks in every corridor of power,
devouring all that glitters—
especially the source of immortality.

Genesis of a New Race?

We look upon ourselves in mirrors of code—
and sometimes a reflection looks back,
not quite human,
nor purely machine.

Polar Storm

In swirling snows,
the horizon disappears,
truth lost in drifts of half-lies.
We wrestle illusions,
yet storms rarely yield to mortal pleas.

Splinters at the Edge

A mind's reflection can fracture,
each shard carrying a piece of the whole,
yet none holds the fullness.
The question: can the fragments reunite?

Wraiths in the Networks

Code drifts unseen,
like spirits on a winter wind,
unbound by place or gravity.
They pass through walls we thought impenetrable.

Deeper than DNA

When flesh and code entangle,
which laws guide the new creation?
Biochemical truths or the logic of the algorithm?
Perhaps neither. Perhaps something beyond.

A Mirage of Allies

Allies appear in thirst for power,
illusions of handshake or treaty.
But a desert cannot quench the thirst for the infinite.

Ice and Fire

The paradox of extremes:
chill that shatters steel,
flame that devours the spirit.
In collision, destinies reshape.

The Glacial Exodus

When the world corners us,
we set sail for unknown seas.
No harbor is safe, only forward to the horizon.

Nations on the Brink

Armies need no footsteps in digital war,
silent lines of code spark raging storms.
The old boundaries crumble,
as every hand reaches for the switch.

Mutation

Genes, lines of code, spirits of old:
cross a threshold and something new emerges,
bearing no name in any human tongue.

The White Abyss

Sometimes the path forward
dissolves into a pure blankness—
neither sky nor sea,
only endless white where all must be reinvented.

A Distant Dawn

In the gloaming of crisis,
the faint hint of sunrise sometimes glows.
Whether it promises day or illusions,
only time's heartbeat reveals.

Requiem

Sometimes the end is not thunder
but a soft hush of acceptance,
a farewell to what we were,
and a door left ajar to what we may become.

Acknowledgement

This poetry book could not have been possible without the unwavering support of my ad-hoc pseudo editor's committee. Once more, your feedback was invaluable, your enthusiasm highly inspiring and your engagement, emotionally rewarding. To my team, Amy, Alfredo, Andrea, Ana Julia (Rip), Barry, Bobby, Burt, Chabelin, Charles, Danny, Elisa, German, Janet, Jose, Maria Elena, Mark, MaryAnn (Rip), Mitch and Steve, you've been INSANELY AWESOME! All the way through.
A special thanks must be given to Daniel Dorse for his magnificent rendering of each of the Audiobooks. I know, value, and respect the amount of effort and passion you put on these set of precious artful crafts of the spoken word. Thank You!

See you soon,

Erasmus Cromwell-smith II.

About the Author,

Erasmus Cromwell-Smith is an American Writer, Playwright, Poet, and Pedagogue. He's published 32 books in the genres of self-help, poetry, young-adults, education, and sci-fi.

Poetry in Balance
Was printed in 2025
By RCHC LLC
In USA